Success in Literacy Reading Tests

UNDERSTANDING
YEAR 7
COMPREHENSION

Excellent for all Students, Teachers, Coaches and Parents

Authors

Alan Horsfield   *M.Ed., B.A., B.Ed., Dip.Sch.Admin., TESOL, Teaching Cert.*
Alan Horsfield has more than 35 years teaching experience in state and private schools in New South Wales and International Schools in Papua New Guinea. He was employed by UNSW (EAA) as an English Research Officer involved in the construction of school tests for English and Mathematics. Alan is a published writer of children's fiction, educational material and school texts.

Elaine Horsfield   *M.A. (Theatre Studies), B.A. (Theatre Media), Teaching Cert.*
Elaine Horsfield has more than 25 years teaching experience in Primary Schools both with the New South Wales Department of Education and in International Schools in Papua New Guinea. She worked with secondary students as coordinator of the NSW Talent Development Project. Elaine is a published writer of children's poetry and educational books.

Editor:
Warwick Marlin B.Sc. Dip.Ed.

Publisher:
Five Senses Education
ABN: 16 001 414437
2/195 Prospect Highway
Seven Hills NSW Australia 2147
sevenhills@fivesenseseducation.com.au
www.fivesenseseducation.com.au

Trade Enquiries:
Phone (02) 9838 9265
Fax (02) 9838 8982
Email: fsonline@fivesenseseducation.com.au

Understanding Year 7 Comprehension
ISBN: 978-1-76032-021-8
1ˢᵗ Edition: April 2015
Copyright: Alan Horsfield © Five Senses Education Pty. Ltd. © Warwick Marlin

AUTHOR'S ACKNOWLEDGEMENTS

Warwick Marlin, my editor, whose advice and guidance have been very much appreciated.

Roger Furniss, at Five Senses Education for publishing my books.

And above all, to **Jones**, my typesetter, for a high standard of typesetting, layout and artwork. A very special thank you for your time, patience, attention to detail, and overall quality of your work.

PARENTS

This book tells you what the teacher often does not have the time to explain in detail - the intricacies of a wide variation in text types and the testing strategies used by Australian testing institutions to assess progress in Literacy. It will give you confidence to support your children by reinforcing what is being taught in schools and what is being tested, especially Reading Comprehension.

TEACHERS

This book introduces text types and test question types Australian students should understand to maximise internal and external Reading Tests. Reading tests may involve comprehension as well as related grammar questions. It eliminates the need to wade through lengthy curriculum documents and it provides a clear, easy to follow format for teachers to use. Teachers can confidently recommend this book to parents as it supports classroom activities and exercises and the Australian Curriculum.

B. Ed., Dip. Ed. PRIMARY SCHOOL TEACHERS

This book contains a variety of recognised school text types with question sets that will improve reading comprehension and improve results in reading tests. It acts as a quick reference book for teachers in the early years of teaching, when there is so much to learn.

"Anyone who says they have only one life to live must not know how to read a book."

Unknown

Understanding Year 7 Comprehension
A. Horsfield © Five Senses Education © W. Marlin

AVAILABILITY OF MATHEMATICS BOOKS

All of the Mathematics books below have been produced by the same editor and publisher, and in many cases the same author (Warwick Marlin). Therefore they all incorporate the same high presentation and philosophy. They can be purchased directly from Five Senses Education, but they are also available in most educational bookshops throughout NSW and Australia (and also some selected bookshops in New Zealand).

New National Curriculum titles

The eight school titles listed directly below have been rewritten and updated in recent years to closely follow the New National Curriculum. **'All levels'** means that the books have been written for students of most ability groups (weak, average and gifted). The graded tests at the end of each chapter ensure that students of most ability groups are extended to their full potential.

❑	YEAR 1	ALL LEVELS
❑	YEAR 2	ALL LEVELS
❑	YEAR 3	ALL LEVELS
❑	YEAR 4	ALL LEVELS
❑	YEAR 5	ALL LEVELS
❑	YEAR 6	ALL LEVELS
❑	YEAR 7	ALL LEVELS
❑	YEAR 8	ALL LEVELS

Other titles in this series

The titles listed below are also available, but they will be fully updated during 2014 and 2015 to also closely follow the new curriculum. However, in the meantime, please note, that these books still adequately address the main features of the new syllabus. We firmly believe that the major topics explained in these titles, and our user friendly presentation and development of the different topics, will always continue to form the vital foundations for all future study and applications of mathematics. This is especially so for the titles up to, and including, Year 10 Advanced.

❑	YEAR 9 & 10	INTERMEDIATE
❑	YEAR 9 & 10	ADVANCED
❑	YEAR 11 & 12	GENERAL MATHS
❑	YEAR 11	EXTENSION 1
❑	YEAR 12	EXTENSION 1

Also by the same Author and Editor (Warwick Marlin)

❑	ESSENTIAL EXERCISES YEAR 1	ALL LEVELS
❑	ESSENTIAL EXERCISES YEAR 2	ALL LEVELS
❑	ESSENTIAL EXERCISES YEAR 3	ALL LEVELS
❑	ESSENTIAL EXERCISES YEAR 4	ALL LEVELS
❑	ESSENTIAL EXERCISES YEAR 5	ALL LEVELS
❑	ESSENTIAL EXERCISES YEAR 6	ALL LEVELS

Developed & written in 2012, this excellent new series of books closely follows the Australian National Curriculum.

CONTENTS

Year 7 Comprehension Passages and Exercises

"So it is with children who learn to read fluently and well. They begin to take flight into whole new worlds as effortlessly as young birds take to the sky."

William James

Understanding Year 7 Comprehension
A. Horsfield © Five Senses Education © W. Marlin

UNDERSTANDING YEAR 7 ENGLISH TESTING

For all Australian students this is their first year in high school. Year 7 is also a NAPLAN year. Groundwork commenced and developed in primary years leads to a more formal understanding of literacy and the concepts that contribute to meaning gleaned from the written word. It is a time when the student is becoming more independent and must accept greater responsibility for his/her progress. It is still important that the home maintains a positive attitude to school and education. The move from primary school to high school should be without anxiety. High schools are more subject-orientated than primary schools. Even though 'homework' will take more and more of the student's time, parents still need to provide positive support that stimulates interest and confidence in reading and writing. The wider the literacy experiences the student has, the more realistic and practical will be the student's appreciation of the written word during high school years. The student will move through high school years ready for new challenges.

Through the first high school year the student will continue to move from a more literal comprehension of text to an interpretive understanding of a wider variety of text types. What is implied becomes more and more important. Making rational judgements from various texts will be a developing skill. This transition will vary from student to student. At times, we all interpret text differently. It is also important to understand that we don't necessarily grasp the intended meaning on a first reading. Re-reading is an important strategy.

Remember: Do not have unreal expectations of what your child can read. Don't 'push' too hard, especially with the more formal written work. Keep literacy fun, especially in reading and then attitudes will be positive. At times it is fun to read something that is not so challenging!

The best way to succeed in any test is to practice.
An old Chinese proverb sums it up well:

> I hear, I forget;
> I see, I remember;
> I do, I understand.

I enjoy a little bit of recreational reading every day!

The NAPLAN testing program for Australian Schools treats three strands of English.
Reading tests, which include the comprehension of a variety of text types,
Writing tests, which focus on writing a narrative, a persuasive text or a recount,
Language Conventions tests, which include Spelling, Punctuation and Grammar.

All three strands are interrelated in the 'real world'. As the National Curriculum states, "Teaching and learning programs should balance and integrate all three strands" (see: http://www.australiancurriculum.edu.au/Year7). The 'interpretation' of digital text becomes increasingly important and relevant. Visual texts also have a place.

This book is based on Year levels not Stages. Year 7 and Year 8 make up Stage 4*. In Year 7 there is a strong emphasis on comprehending a variety of text types of increasing difficulty and subtlety. Not all text types get the same attention. The study of persuasive text is more complex and subtle than, say, following directions. As families and society are a complex mix of differing experiences, children will have different exposure to different text types. Individual children will develop different strengths and weaknesses.

This book focuses specifically on Reading but the skills learned in Reading can assist in the development of the child's Writing skills. The skills learned in the Language Convention strand can improve both Reading and Writing.

We have included a Literacy Tip (Lit Tip) component at the end of each set of questions. These may help with any Language Convention questions that come up in standardised reading tests as well adding 'tricks' that may improve the quality of Writing test responses.
*See:http://syllabus.bos.nsw.edu.au/stages/

HOW TO USE THIS BOOK EFFECTIVELY

As stated, this book's primary aim is to improve Reading comprehension with some input into Language Conventions. Obviously the Speaking, Listening and Handwriting strands are not included.

The passages are not selected in any specific order but are intended to present a wide variation of text types. Those most likely to be part of the testing situation are treated more often. The text type is shown at the top of each passage as well as in the **List of comprehension passages and exercises** chart that follows.

There will be differences of focus from school to school, as teachers tend to select topics in varying sequences according to their program at a particular time in the year. Some students may also be involved in accelerated promotion, enrichment or remedial activities.

ABOUT THE EXERCISES

The intent of the 40 passages is to provide one passage per week for each school week. This should not impinge too much on the increasingly heavy obligations sets by the school/class teacher for homework and research. There is one easier **practice passage** provided to make the child aware of a range of question types that may be encountered.

Children need not work through the exercisers from 1 to 40 in the order in which they are presented in this book. There is the option of practicing a particular text type, e. g. poetry.

The Comprehension Answers and the Lit Tip Answers are on separate pages at the back of the book.

Reading texts can be based on either **Factual** or **Literary** texts.
Year 7 question types often include the skills of:

- **Locating** such things as information, a sequence of events, literary techniques, grammar conventions and vocabulary features,

- **Identifying** genres, the purpose of a text, literary techniques, appropriate punctuation, word meanings,

- **Interpreting** visual information, multiple pieces of information, language style,

- **Inferring** next events in a text, reasons for a character's action, outcomes, the effect of tense and person, and

- **Synthesising** the tone of a text, the main idea in a text, a character's motivation, the writer's opinion, the intended audience for a text.

These above skills are more or less arranged in an order of difficulty.

Alan Horsfield M.Ed., B.A., B.Ed., Dip.Sch.Admin., TESOL, Teaching Cert.
Elaine Horsfield M. A. (Theatre Studies), B. A. (Theatre Media), Teaching Cert.

Understanding Year 7 Comprehension
A. Horsfield © Five Senses Education © W. Marlin

TEST SOURCES

The questions, information and practice provided by this book will benefit the student sitting for the following tests.

Externally produced tests

NAPLAN (National Assessment - Literacy and Numeracy) Used Australia wide.
PAT (-R) (Progressive Achievements Tests - Reading)
ICAS (International Competitions and Assessments for Schools) Run by EAA.
Selective schools and High Schools Placement Tests (Most states have tests specific to that state's educational policy.)
Scholarship Tests
ACER (Australian Council for Educational Research) Scholarship tests (Most states have tests specific to that state's educational policy)
AusVELS (Australian Curriculum in Victoria Essential Learning Standards)
Independent Assessment Agencies (e.g. Academic Assessment Services)
ISA (International Schools Assessment) run by ACER

There may be a number of other independent, external sources for literacy testing.

School produced tests

year tests
class tests
school tests

Information provided in this book may also be beneficial in certain competitions run by commercial enterprises.

A number of commercial publishers also provide books of practice tests.

The purpose of testing

Testing has a variety of purposes and the purpose will often determine the type of test administered. Tests may be used to
- determine what the student has learned
- rank students in order of ability
- select the most worthy student for a school or class
- determine the strength and weakness of classroom teaching
- determine any 'short-comings' in a school's educational program
- ascertain the effectiveness of certain teaching strategies
- evaluate the effectiveness of departmental/official syllabuses

The Australian Curriculum (http://www.australiancurriculum.edu.au/Year7) states the Year 7 students should be able to:
- Identify and explore ideas and viewpoints about events, issues and characters represented in texts drawn from different historical, social and cultural contexts(ACELT 1619),
- Reflect on ideas and opinions about characters, settings and events in literary texts, identifying areas of agreement and difference with others and justifying a point of view(ACELT 1620),
- Compare the ways that language and images are used to create character, and to influence emotions and opinions in different types of texts(ACELT 1621),
- Discuss aspects of texts, for example their aesthetic and social value, using relevant and appropriate metalanguage(ACELT 1803),
- Recognise and analyse the ways that characterisation, events and settings are combined in narratives, and discuss the purposes and appeal of different approaches(ACELT 1622),
- Understand, interpret and discuss how language is compressed to produce a dramatic effect in film or drama, and to create layers of meaning in poetry, for example haiku, tankas, couplets, free verse and verse novels(ACELT 1623).

A BRIEF SUMMARY OF SOME QUESTION FORMATS AND STYLES.

Read the opinions expressed in **The zoo debate** as the text for a set of questions.

FOR ZOOS It is claimed that animals don't have rights as people do. It follows that in order to protect certain species they need to be captured or rescued and confined to secure environments. Wildlife poaching for ivory, fur, hides and dubious 'medicines' continues regardless of international treaties banning it. Zoos are an option - a haven for saving and breeding of endangered wild animals for future _____(4)_____. Zoos have safe cages.

AGAINST ZOOS Regardless of how good facilities in a zoo are, animals are in prisons. Animals suffer when confined to a cage! Their natural movements are not bounded by fences. Their feeding behaviour is determined by humans not by natural instincts and skills. These skills are lost. Released animals rarely survive long in their so-called natural environment. It is a foreign land.

Zoos are nothing more than a recreational pleasure for families with very little educational benefit.

Adapted from an idea in: http://www.buzzle.com/articles/pros-and-cons-of-zoos.html

---

Many tests are based on multiple-choice responses. You are most often given a choice of four possible answers (options) to choose from. Options may be in a vertical or horizontal format.
Some will take the form of a question: You may have to circle a letter or shade a box.

1. Who will benefit in the long term by keeping animals in zoos?
   A   zoo staff
   B   poachers
   C   educators
   D   future generations

> The question could have been framed so that you have to complete a sentence.

2. The long-term benefits of keeping animals in zoos will be for
   A   zoo staff   B   poachers
   C   educators   D   future generations

Some questions may have to do with a word or phrase meanings.
3. Choose the word that could best replace species as used in the text.
   A   kinds   B   makes   C   specialists   D   groups

4. Which word would best go in the space labelled (4)?
   A   investments   B   closures   C   generations   D   visits

Some questions are called *free response questions*. You will have to write an answer.
5. Who benefits illegally from wild animals? _____(Write your answer on the line.)

Sometimes you might have to decide if something is TRUE or FALSE.
6. Tick the box to show if this statement is TRUE or FALSE.

   Animals are often poached for medical reasons.   TRUE ☐   FALSE ☐

There will be times when you will have to read the whole text and make a judgement.
7. What are the two writers most concerned about in their writing?
   A   how to prevent poaching   B   the benefits of caging animals
   C   the importance of breeding programs   D   the cost of feeding zoo animals

8. There might be a question about the use of language in the text.
   The sentence, *It is a foreign land*, is an example of a
   A   metaphor   B   simile   C   hyperbole

9. You might have to decide if, according to the text, a statement is FACT or OPINION.
   Are the words, *Zoos have safe cages*, fact or opinion? _____(Write your answer here.)

You may have to make a judgement about character or their motives.
10. Which word best describes how the **AGAINST** writer feel about the zoo issue?
   A   incensed   B   passionate   C   confused   D   worried

11. Sometimes you might have to work out the sequence in which events occurred, and use numbers to show the correct sequence. (This passage does not lend itself to sequencing questions.)

Answers: 1. D, 2. D,   3. A,   4. C,   5.poachers   6. TRUE,   7. B,   8. A (metaphor)   9.FACT   10.B

Understanding Year 7 Comprehension
A. Horsfield © Five Senses Education © W. Marlin

This is a practice page. (The answers follow the questions)

Read the narrative **The Cave Dwellers.**

The Cave Dwellers

Ubet made his way through the dank-smelling streets to his cave, his fish bouncing against his side. He passed a large square excavation in the sandstone bedrock. The grey-yellow walls were vertical and quite smooth. The pit contained a pool of brown, slimy water. In the water were the <u>flotsam and jetsam</u> of another time that always left Ubet wondering. Twisted metal scaffolding protruded from the water at weird angles. Many times, an adventurous youngun had been found floating in the sinister water.

Ubet looked at the City buildings with much the same eye a medieval Egyptian peasant may have looked at the Pyramids. They were there, always there, like the stars.

Ubet felt pangs of thirst. Salt air always made him thirsty. He suppressed a cough and scratched irritably at his lank and thinning hair.

A mutantcat scurried awkwardly across the street, <u>yowling</u>. Ubet couldn't tell if it was horribly deformed or if it had been savagely attacked. He looked to where it had come from. He knew they avoided being alone in the open. A small pack of mutantrats was dragging the remains of a bloodied mutantcat down an open storm water shaft. He could see it had been diseased. Its body was thin and wasted. He had seen such animals before. They had little energy and little drive to survive. They had no fight.

The mutantrats eyed Ubet suspiciously but they showed no fear. He feared they were becoming more daring, or more desperate.

Further on Ubet could see The Hills through gaps in the crumbling buildings and derelict towers. The hills of Paddington and Randwick. And some whose names had been forgotten. He was vaguely aware that so much had been forgotten. He thought of Boy for a moment.

It was unconfirmed knowledge that there were sti̲̲le shelters in barricaded streets. Walls had been built across streets to keep the tribes out but the City tribes rarely went there. More importantly the walls were to give some protection from the marauding Gangs from the nearby dens in Surry. These Gangs had little fear but rarely ventured into the City to plunder or kill. They got their pleasure elsewhere.

The most feared group was the small, but vicious Kings Cross Gang.

From: *The Mutants* by A. Horsfield

Understanding Narratives

Circle a letter to answer questions 1 to 8.

(**Note:** The answers follow the questions for this Practice passage.)

1. What was Ubet most likely doing before he passed by the excavation?
    A   looking for Boy
    B   fishing in the sea
    C   searching for mutantrats
    D   avoiding marauding gangs

2. What activity was the mutantcat most likely engaged in?
    A   hunting for a feed of mutantrats
    B   preparing to attack Ubet
    C   escaping to the nearby hills
    D   avoiding a pack of mutantrats

3. As used in the text, what does *flotsam and jetsam* (paragraph 1) refer to?
    A   debris   B   junk   C   residue   D   waste

4. The words, *Ubet looked at the City buildings with much the same eye a medieval Egyptian peasant may have looked at the Pyramids*, is an example of
    A   a simile   B   a metaphor
    C   an analogy   D   hyperbole (an exaggeration)

5. The mutantcat was *yowling* (paragraph 3). This suggests the mutantcat was
    A   growling softly in fear
    B   whimpering quietly
    C   snarling defensively
    D   howling in distress

6. The title of the extract suggests the passage is about
    A   people who have reverted to a primitive state
    B   the survival skills of ancient people
    C   cave explorers from a another city
    D   the evolution of apes to humans

7. From the reader's perspective this passage is written as if set in the
    A   past   B   present   C   future

8. The text is most likely intended to create a feeling of
    A   excitement   B   despair
    C   frivolity   D   calm

Answers: 1. B   2. D   3. A   4. C   5. D   6. A   7. C   8. B

Understanding Year 7 Comprehension
A. Horsfield © Five Senses Education © W. Marlin

Year 7 Comprehension Passages and Exercises

Each of the 40 passages has a set of eight questions - comprehension and language questions,based upon that text. Following the questions is a section called **Lit Tip** (short for Literacy Tips). These are gems of information that are intended to develop the child's responses to Language Conventions questions arising in texts and tests. They may also be beneficial when answering questions in Language Convention (Grammar) papers or when completing Writing assessment tasks.

Understanding Year 7 Comprehension
A. Horsfield © Five Senses Education © W. Marlin

Read the recount **_Deep Beyond the Reef._**

Deep Beyond the Reef

(Owen Scott lived with his family in Fiji and remembers life there in the middle of last century.)

As well as the arrival of the butcher, every day the Chinese market gardeners would bring fresh vegetables to the house. Both would take their produce separately to the back door. Fish caught in Laucala Bay was also brought to the back door.

Everything had to be covered against flies. Whatever you were drinking had a little fly cover over it, with beads that hung around the edge that tinkled against the side of the glass. In the fly season it was almost impossible to get food from plate to mouth. That was a practical reason why servants manned the punkahs (mechanical fans) in the tropics, however distasteful such an image of servitude is today. Even with punkahs, you also had to personally fan the fork from plate to mouth.

There were two other methods of dealing with the flies. Tapes were hung from the ceiling of the kitchen with a substance that attracted flies to it. At night they rested there. Before the servants left each day, long thin calico bags were carefully slipped up the tapes and tied at the top. The bags were then plunged into boiling water.

The other method involved a machine that my father thought came from Germany. It was a small box, inside of which was a barrel with indentions, like waves, where honey or jam was put. The barrel revolved very slowly when wound up. The flies stuck to the honey or jam and were then knocked off the barrel into a little pan of water placed underneath. As a child, my uncle Maurice used to watch this contraption for hours.

Considering the tropical heat, the flies and the lack of modern refrigeration the meals prepared by my grandmother were_____(8)_____.

Many thanks to Owen Scott for permission to use this text.
From: Deep Beyond the Reef by Owen Scott 2004 Penguin Books pp. 51, 52

Understanding Recounts

Circle a letter to answer questions 1 to 8.

1. The flies became a problem for the Scott family while in Fiji
   - A when fishermen delivered fish to the backdoor
   - B after the servants had left the house for the evening
   - C in one particular season of each year
   - D when the grandmother was cooking one of the meals

2. Why did the writer state: *it was almost impossible to get food from plate to mouth?*
   - A the flies were a menace in their relentlessness
   - B the servants manning the punkahs were careless
   - C the beads on the food covers made eating awkward
   - D the quality of the delivered food was detestable

3. Look at the photo.
   The purpose of the beads on the jug cover is to
   - A make the cover attractive
   - B provide soothing tinkling sounds
   - C scare off flies
   - D hold the cover in place

4. How did Maurice react to the fly trapping contraption?
   - A He was fascinated by it.
   - B He was disgusted by it.
   - C He was appalled by it.
   - D He was puzzled by it.

5. The flies settled on the tapes hanging from the ceiling because
   - A it meant they were closer to a possible source of food
   - B they were attracted by the substances spread on the tapes
   - C it was a safe place to avoid being struck by the mechanical fans
   - D they were less likely to be killed by servants while on the tapes

6. The attitude of the Scott family to the non-Europeans was one of
   - A distrust
   - B ridicule
   - C superiority
   - D admiration

7. What was the most likely power source for the contraption for catching flies?
   - A electricity
   - B clockwork
   - C hand
   - D wind

8. A word has been deleted from the text.
   Which word would be best suited to the space (8)?
   - A tasteless
   - B bearable
   - C meagre
   - D legendary

Lit Tip 1 - Improve your Literacy skills   **Than or then**

Than and then are often mispronounced in spoken English.

Than can be used as a preposition to introduce a comparison.

Example: The father was much shorter than his son.

It can also be used as a conjunction: He watches rather than plays.

Then is an adverb: I won some money then I lost it!

Circle the word that correctly completes these sentences. Give their part of speech.

1. Sam was always helpful, (than, then) something happened. _____

2. Jan doesn't know any more (than, then) I do! _____

3

Understanding Year 7 Comprehension
A. Horsfield © Five Senses Education © W. Marlin

2 Read the report *Green Ants in North Queensland.*

Green Ants in North Queensland

Now if you thought life was busy – you haven't seen anything until you've seen a green ants nest in full defence mode! They clamber all over the tree containing their nest and protect it from invaders with a fervour and ferocity only to be attributed to the Mongol hordes. These ants are often found in the fruiting trees of Far North Queensland. When an unsuspecting forager tries to help themselves to some tasty fruit, they find themselves attacked by a formidable miniature army of

slicing and slashing mandibles – and who could blame them! Their bite is not very painful but several ants attacking simultaneously can be a touch uncomfortable.

The nests are large and built by sticking the leaves at the end of branches together to create a sort of globular home.

Most of the nest construction and weaving is conducted at night with major workers weaving towards the exterior of the nests and minor workers weaving within the interior.

A mature colony of green tree ants can hold as many as 100 000 to 500 000 workers and a colony may span as many as 12 trees and contain as many as 150 nests. Green ant colonies have one queen and a colony can live for up to eight years. Minor workers usually remain within the egg chambers of the nest tending the larvae; whereas major workers defend the colony territory, and assist with the care of the queen and forage.

Now the numbers don't always have it. There are sneaky spiders like the Salticidae spiders, or jumping spiders, as they are sometimes referred to, which have excellent eyesight and are only active during daylight. They weave a protective silken cocoon in which to spend the night. Interestingly, this spider does not look like a green ant but instead the fiendish arthropod chemically mimics green tree ants, affectively disguised as an ant it sneaks into the green ants nest, bluffs it's way into the nursery and feeds on their larvae. Green ants don't have good vision and circumnavigate their surroundings by scent, smelling everything with their antennae. Consequently, the ants think the spider is another ant and ignore its presence within the nest.

Now is it any wonder green ants are pretty intolerant of any invasion into their territory.

My thanks to Thala Beach resort for permission to use this information.
Source: http://www.thalabeach.com.au/green-ants-australia/

Understanding Reports

Circle a letter or write an answer for questions 1 to 8.

1. The main defence green ants have is
   - A   the fortifications in their nests
   - B   their ability to attack in numbers
   - C   the venom in their sting
   - D   their objectionable smell

2. Green ant nests are described as *sort of globular?*
   This means the nests are
   - A   sticky to touch
   - B   found worldwide
   - C   spherical in shape
   - D   big and spongy

3. The *mandibles* refer to the green ant's
   - A   jaws
   - B   sting
   - C   legs
   - D   feelers

4. According to the text which statement is CORRECT?
   - A   The major green ant workers care for the larvae in the nest.
   - B   The jumping spider looks like a green ant.
   - C   A single green ant bite can be quite painful.
   - D   There is more than one nest in a green ant colony.

5. How does the jumping spider avoid being caught in the green ants' nest?
   - A   it mimics the smell of the green ants
   - B   it sneaks in at night
   - C   it attacks any ant that tries to stop it
   - D   it pretends to be a minor worker

6. How does the writer feel about green ants?
   - A   He finds them fearsome.
   - B   He worries about their destruction of trees.
   - C   He admires their resourcefulness.
   - D   He thinks they are amusing.

7. These words: *with a fervour and ferocity only to be attributed to the Mongol hordes*
   is an example of
   - A   a simile
   - B   a metaphor
   - C   a euphemism
   - D   an analogy

8. For how long might a green ant colony survive?
   Write your answer on the line. _____

Lit Tip 2 – Improve your Literacy skills   Irregular plurals
Generally to make a plural noun (or singular verb) you add s (or *es* or (i)*es*).
Some nouns have unusual (irregular) plurals: radius/radii, calf/calves, foot/feet
(You may check with a reference source.)

What is the plural for: life _____, ox _____, person _____

Try these: penny _____, datum _____, sheep, _____, louse _____

mother-in-law, _____, basis _____, deer _____

What is the singular for: children _____, crises _____, fungi _____

Understanding Year 7 Comprehension
A. Horsfield © Five Senses Education © W. Marlin

Bosley

Bosley was getting fed up with his home.
The food was an utter disgrace.
They fed him with fish that came out of a tin
Of a quality really just fit for the bin.
And he knew he was getting decidedly thin,
So he set out to find a new place.

He followed his nose till he came to a street
That sent him right into a spin.
For the smells that were wafting from each café door,
Were a promise that wonderful meals were in store.
And the growl in his stomach became a loud roar!
So he opened a door and went in.

It wasn't the place for a cat like himself
He thought, as he flew out the door.
For the waiter who'd stepped on his serpentine tail
Had dropped all the food, as he let out a wail,
And the diners who sat there were looking quite pale,
Not to mention the dreadful décor!

Undeterred by his first relocation attempt,
Bosley's nose told him where next to look.
This time as he stopped by a Sea Food Café
He knew that he'd found where he wanted to stay.
So he opened the door without further delay
And presented himself to the cook.

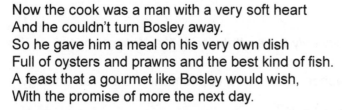

Now the cook was a man with a very soft heart
And he couldn't turn Bosley away.
So he gave him a meal on his very own dish
Full of oysters and prawns and the best kind of fish.
A feast that a gourmet like Bosley would wish,
With the promise of more the next day.

But back at his home things were really quite grim
For his owners were missing their pet.
And they'd printed up posters to put round the street
With a picture of Bosley, angelic and sweet.
And a promise to serve him the very best meat
If he'd only forgive and forget.

So Bosley the cat now has visiting rights
At the Sea Food Café up the way.
Though he spends winter nights on a rug by the fire
And his owners give in to his every desire,
He can often be seen strolling up to inquire
What the café is serving today.

Elaine Horsfield

Understanding Poetry

Circle a letter to answer questions 1 to 8.

1. Bosley's venture into the street was occasioned by his
   - A need to prevent starvation
   - B desire for quality food
   - C wish to find a place to live
   - D love of outdoor living

2. According to the poem which statement is CORRECT?
   - A Bosley was a neglected cat.
   - B Bosley didn't enjoy seafood.
   - C Bosley felt fearful in the street.
   - D Bosley was not deterred by failure.

3. Bosley could best be described as being
   - A self-assertive
   - B feint-heated
   - C adaptable
   - D deprived

4. Which technique does the poet use in the words *He followed his nose*?
   - A a simile
   - B an idiom
   - C alliteration
   - D onomatopoeia

5. In stanza 5 the poet uses the word *gourmet* to emphasise the
   - A amount of food Bosley would require
   - B mismatch between what Bosley was given and what he ate
   - C quality of food Bosley was prepared to accept
   - D flavour of tin fish Bosley was given to eat

6. What did Bosley's owners do to encourage him to come home?
   - A they got in extra supplies of tin-fish cat food
   - B they purchased food from the Sea Food Café
   - C they allowed Bosley to have nightly visits to cafés in the street
   - D they provided home conditions suitable for a cat of Bosley's status

7. Which word is a suitable synonym for *wafting* as used in the poem?
   - A drifting
   - B sifting
   - C wading
   - D waffling

8. After *his first relocation attempt* Bosley decided to
   - A return to his home
   - B accept meals of tin fish
   - C look for another café
   - D check out posters around the street

Lit Tip 3 – Improve your Literacy skills   **Idiom**

Did you have a problem with question 4?

Idiom is a group of words whose meaning is not obvious from the actual meaning of the words.

Example: a *hot potato* refers to an issue that many people argue about

the *drop of a hat* means to do something without hesitation

Briefly, what is meant by: *hit the nail on the head* _____

hit the sack _____ , *off one's rocker* _____

Understanding Year 7 Comprehension
A. Horsfield © Five Senses Education © W. Marlin

Read the narrative *The Earthquake.*

The Earthquake

On the first day back at school after the term vacation there was an earthquake. Marty had entered the deserted classroom to drop off his bag and then wandered to the back of the room where he was about to straighten a space project display. His group had put it up at the end of the previous term.

First he heard a deep, prolonged rumbling noise that sounded like distant thunder. It got louder. Then the floor beneath his feet began to quiver and shift. For a moment he thought the class next door were all running on the spot. Then he realised that teachers don't allow that sort of thing in classrooms. The thought was silly anyway. There was no class next door. Classes hadn't commenced for the day.

The silliness of this idea had no time to sink in before the floor lurched and heaved and he was thrown sideways across the nearest desk. The rules for remaining upright and balanced no longer existed. The elements were conspiring to shake him off his feet and he couldn't stop them.

The school had an earthquake drill last term but he hadn't really taken much notice. The teachers were in control then and you did as you were told without thinking. He suddenly remembered something about getting under a desk, as the floor seemed to roll like a gentle wave across a pond.

Items was spilling off shelves and crashing to the floor or rolling around like demented ants. Suddenly a side window splintered and glass tumbled to the floor. There was a loud crack above his head. A bookcase crashed to the floor near the door. The door was the only exit.

If the roof caves in you are safer under a desk, he remembered.

Before the next jolt struck he was scrambling under a jiggling desk and hanging onto its legs to stop it from bouncing away.

Another loud, deep crack came from the ceiling. Bits of plaster fell to the floor like hailstones.

In the distance he heard someone shout, "Earthquake!" Then the school emergency siren sounded.

Another tremor and the desk Marty was under tried to dance across the floor.

Then he smelt gas.

Understanding Narratives

Circle a letter to answer questions 1 to 8.

1. What was the first indication Marty had that he might be experiencing an earthquake?
   - A the class next door began running on the spot
   - B he heard a prolonged and distant rumble
   - C the floor began to move under his feet
   - D he saw bits of ceiling plaster falling onto the floor

2. When Marty first entered his classroom he was feeling
   - A wary
   - B confused
   - C excited
   - D relaxed

3. The writer uses a simile to describe the
   - A call of someone's warning cry
   - B movement of the desk during the tremor
   - C items rolling across the floor after spilling off the shelves
   - D noises in the ceiling as the earthquake struck

4. What was the problem Marty discovered with the desk?
   - A the desk kept moving across the floor
   - B the desk provided no protection from a ceiling collapse
   - C the desk was liable to fall over
   - D the desk was too low to hide under

5. What was the last sound Marty heard as he hid under the desk?
   - A an emergency siren
   - B the sound of gas escaping
   - C a bookcase falling over
   - D someone shouting, "Earthquake!"

6. What blocked Marty's escape from the classroom?
   - A the splintered window glass
   - B the moving row of desks
   - C parts of the ceiling falling in
   - D a toppled bookcase

7. Which word from the passage does **not** relate to movement?
   - A quiver
   - B demented
   - C splintered
   - D jiggling

8. The last line, *Then he smelt gas* suggests that
   - A Marty's situation had suddenly got worse
   - B something has spilled when the bookcase collapsed
   - C someone had started cooking
   - D emergency vehicles were in the school grounds

Lit Tip 4 – Improve your Literacy skills   The royal we

Queen Victoria famously once said, 'We are not amused.'
Most people would say, 'I am not amused', but royalty can use the pronoun *we*.
We is used by royalty to indicate they represent both themselves and the people.
Now-a-days it is often used by presidents and prime ministers.
When 'ordinary' people use we they are often being sarcastic - or pompous!

If someone acts **pompously** they think they are _____

Understanding Year 7 Comprehension
A. Horsfield © Five Senses Education © W. Marlin

The Canning Stock Route

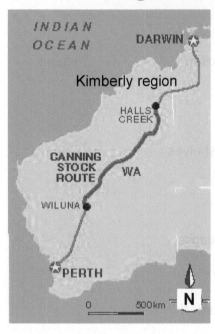

The Canning Stock Route was first proposed by East Kimberley pastoralist James Isdell in 1905. The route, which crossed deserts, had been explored in 1896 but was largely considered an unviable route.

In Western Australia (WA), at the beginning of the 20th century, East Kimberley cattlemen were looking for a way to cross the deserts with their cattle as a way to break a West Kimberley monopoly that controlled beef supplies to Perth and the southern goldfields. The problem for East Kimberley cattlemen was their cattle were infested with ticks which carried malaria-like parasites.

If ticks survived the sea journey to Perth they could spread through southern cattle herds. For the West Kimberley cattlemen the monopoly meant higher returns.

Being an East Kimberley cattleman, James Isdell wanted to break that monopoly. With East Kimberley cattlemen desperate to get their cattle to markets and the WA Government keen for competition to bring beef prices down, the 1905 proposal of a desert stock route, put forward by Isdell, was taken seriously.

Isdell argued ticks would not survive the long journey down the dry stock route. They posed no risk to southern cattle herds. He won the argument and in 1906 the Government appointed Alfred Canning to survey the route. With a team of 23 camels, two horses and eight men Canning took six months to survey a route. He needed enough water along the way for up to 800 head of cattle at a time, and no further than a day's droving apart.

Once the survey had been completed Canning returned with a construction party and from 1908 to 1910 built 51 wells along the route. Commercial droving began in 1910, but the stock route was unpopular.

In 1928 the high beef price in Western Australia led to renewed interest in the stock route. In 1929 William Snell was commissioned to repair the wells and found that the only wells undamaged were the ones Aboriginal people used. In 1930, Canning (aged 70) was asked to help with repairs.

There were only 37 recorded drives down the route, including horse drives. The last run was in 1959.

During WWII (1939–1945) the route was upgraded at huge expense in case an evacuation of northern Australia was required due to a Japanese invasion.

Map Adapted from: www.bizarq.nl/csr/CSRmap.jpg
http://www.outbackspirittours.com.au/destinations/canning-stock-route/

Understanding Recounts

Circle a letter or write an answer for questions 1 to 8.

1. Who did the West Kimberley cattlemen have a dispute with?
   - A   Alfred Canning
   - B   West Australian Government
   - C   James Isdell
   - D   the East Kimberley cattlemen

2. How many recorded drives went down the Canning Stock Route?

   Write your answer in the box. ☐

3. The Canning Stock Route was between the towns of: (Write your answers on the lines)
   _____ and _____

4. When was the Canning Stock Route completed?
   - A   1908
   - B   1910
   - C   1928
   - D   1959

5. Write the numbers 1 to 4 in the boxes to show the correct order in which events occurred in the recount. The first one (1) has been done for you.

☐	commercial droving began along the Canning Stock Route in 1910
☐	a proposal for a stock route was put forward in 1906
☐	repairs were carried out on the route's wells.
1	the stock route was explored in 1896

6. The stock route was reopened after 1939 because
   - A   it could be an escape route in the event of a Japanese attack
   - B   the wells along the route had been restored
   - C   beef prices in Perth had risen drastically
   - D   ticks had infested cattle from the East Kimberley region

7. About how long is the Canning Stock Route?
   - A   100 km
   - B   500 km
   - C   1500 km
   - D   5000 km

8. As a cattleman, James Isdell's ambition was to
   - A   provide tick free cattle for the southern markets
   - B   join the East Kimberley cattlemen's monopoly
   - C   have a quick route for cattle from the north to the south
   - D   open up the southern markets to West Kimberley beef

Lit Tip 5 – Improve your Literacy skills   Shades of meaning

In your writing it is beneficial to get the right shade of meaning.
The word *said* has little impact. Why not try *murmured, claimed* or *suggested.*
There are dozens of *said* type words. Build up a list for your writing tasks.
Here are some '*wept*'- type words: *cried, sobbed, bawled, howled* and *blubbered.*
Choose the best word for the space.
1. The old man _____ quietly when his pet dog died.
2. The baby _____ loudly when he was refused a lolly in the supermarket.

Understanding Year 7 Comprehension
A. Horsfield © Five Senses Education © W. Marlin

Gumleaf Playing

Gumleaf playing has long been linked with Aboriginal players and taught by Aboriginal teachers. There is also a colonial and twentieth century non-Aboriginal tradition of gumleaf playing.

The gumleaf is the most primitive of musical instruments since it consists simply of a leaf from a gumtree.

Start with finding a large, well-formed gum leaf like the one above. With your fingernail, scratch a small piece of the flesh off the leaf from one side, leaving the membrane of the other side exposed. It is slightly transparent if done successfully.

The leaf is held against the lips using the fingers of both hands. With your lips pursed, blow across the exposed membrane to make a sound. Skilled gum leaf players can get simple tunes from the vibrating edge of the membrane.

In normal playing the leaf is held tightly against the lower lip and lightly against the upper lip. It is stretched rather tightly between the two hands. Air blown out of the mouth will lift the top of the leaf away from upper lip allowing the air to escape. In this sense the valve can be described as an "outward-swinging door".

It works in much the same way as that of the valve produced by the lips of a brass-instrument player.

It takes a bit of trial and error for a beginner to even produce a sound from a gumleaf. A skilled player can control the pitch with some accuracy over a range of more than an octave and play simple tunes with ease.

The technique for varying the mouth and vocal tract when playing the gumleaf is similar to that used in whistling.

An alternate method: the leaf is held vertically between the sides of two opposed thumbs, which are pressed against the lips. The resulting sound, while having a greater pitch, is rough and chaotic. It is useful for special effects, such as imitating the squawk of the sulphur-crested cockatoo, but_____(4)_____.

Source (adapted): http://www.didjshop.com/austrAboriginalMusicInstruments.htm

Understanding Procedures

Circle a letter to answer questions 1 to 8.

1. Once a person has found a suitable gumleaf to play they must next
   - A remove some flesh from the leaf
   - B place the leaf across that person's lips
   - C bend the leaf into a lip shape
   - D play a tune with a range of one octave

2. Which word would be a suitable substitute for *skilled* as used in paragraph 7?
   - A trained
   - B accomplished
   - C qualified
   - D cautious

3. Playing a gumleaf is similar in many ways to
   - A playing in a band
   - B making scratching sounds
   - C imitating cockatoos
   - D whistling

4. The final words have been deleted from the text.
   Which words would be best suited to the space (4)?
   - A has no obvious musical value
   - B can attract cockatoos to homes
   - C has no place in the average home
   - D can scare off small predators

5. The word scratch as used in the text (paragraph 2) is a
   - A noun
   - B adjective
   - C verb
   - D article

6. *Lips pursed* (paragraph 3) are lips that
   - A form a circle
   - B are puckered
   - C have the corners turned up
   - D become flattened

7. A gum leaf played with the leaf in a vertical position to the mouth would be
   - A tuneful
   - B muted
   - C irritating
   - D soothing

8. Who is most likely to benefit most from this information?
   - A people with an Aboriginal heritage
   - B professional musicians
   - C the owners of gumtree plantations
   - D people happy to experiment with sounds

Lit Tip 6 – Improve your literacy skills   **Euphemisms**

A **euphemism** is a nice way of saying something that may be considered unpleasant or embarrassing. We say someone is *between* jobs instead of saying *out of work*.
Common euphemisms: *restroom* - lavatory, *correction facility* - prison, *big boned* - fat
Complete these with a more direct word.
Euphemisms aren't always polite.

1. A man who is *thin* on top is _____.
2. *Croaked* means someone _____ .
3. What is a euphemism your family uses for a *doctor*? _____

Understanding Year 7 Comprehension
A. Horsfield © Five Senses Education © W. Marlin

Terms for Dying

To die or not to die - is that the question? How should we respond to dying? We all have our own strategies. But what is wrong with saying died or dead?

Why do we avoid the deadly 'D' word? It's time people faced up to the cold hard truth and say so-and-so died rather than trying to give death the sugar coated pill.

Somewhere in the last century people stopped dying. People and sometimes animals, do a variety of other things than dying. If one is to truthfully say so-and-so died we are regarded as being insensitive!

People now are passing away, passing on and sometimes passing over. When you think about it logically these terms have little meaning. Where are the deceased passing on to or over to? Instead of dying are they getting involved in some vague avoidance of death.

Of course, in jest and away from the bereaved family and friends, we have some pretty interesting euphemisms: on the other side, gone to join his/her maker and he/she is no longer with us.

We could be less polite and say kicked the bucket, pushing up daisies, visited by the grim reaper and bit the dust.

We could be quite crass with such terms as belly up, karked it and flat-lined.

Such 'unrelated' terms can cause communication problems. There's a story about little Johnny asking his grandfather if he can make a frog sound. The grandfather asks why. Little Johnny tells him that his parents said they can go to Disneyland once grandpa croaks!

Surely it is better to face the fact and come to terms with the truth, gain closure and let grief run its full course? Death is, after all, a natural part of life. It's time to stop pulling punches and stop using clichés and euphemisms to avoid saying death and dying. It doesn't bring the person back. Death is permanent.

As Woody Allen said, "I'm not afraid of death; I just don't want to be there when it happens."

From: an idea in the SMH 9 August 2014 by Virginia Howard.
Euphemisms by John Ayto Bloomsbury Publishing, England 1993.

1. What does the writer of the text feel strongly about?
    - A   that death is so permanent
    - B   people making jokes about death
    - C   the use of insensitive words for death
    - D   attempts to protect people from the reality of death

2. Which *death* term would be most upsetting to a recently bereaved person?
    - A   on the other side
    - B   kicked the bucket
    - C   joined his maker
    - D   no longer with us

3. Which literary device does the writer use in paragraph 1?
    - A   rhetorical questions
    - B   euphemisms
    - C   a metaphor
    - D   personification

4. How does the writer feel about people who avoid saying *death*?
    - A   They must be very sensible and considerate people.
    - B   They have a communication problem.
    - C   They should face up to the truth and be realistic.
    - D   They have no understanding of the permanence of death.

5. The term *sugar coated pill* (paragraph 2) refers to
    - A   telling lies about a person who has died
    - B   making something bad seem less unpleasant
    - C   hiding the truth from those who feel bereaved
    - D   confusing mourners about what has really happened

6. **Tone** is the author's attitude toward the topic. (Check out **Lit Tip 8** for help.)
    The writer, in **Terms for Dying**, is being
    - A   flippant
    - B   sombre
    - C   entertaining
    - D   callous

7. Which word would be a suitable replacement for *crass* as used in the text?
    - A   critical
    - B   croak
    - C   loud
    - D   insensitive

8. What does the second last paragraph suggest about Johnny's parents?
    - A   they were due for an inheritance
    - B   they wanted to take Grandpa to Disneyland
    - C   they thought Johnny was being rude to Grandpa
    - D   they didn't know much about frogs

Lit Tip 7 – Improve your literacy skills   Rhetorical questions

Did you have a problem with Q 3? Here's some help.
Although they are not intended to be answered, rhetorical questions are meant to get the reader's (or listener's) attention and to start thinking. The person asking mostly knows the answer he/she wants.
Examples: It's hot today, isn't it?   Can't you do anything right?
If someone asks, *"Do pigs fly?"* what do they mean? _____
Rhetorical questions are a clever technique to use in persuasive writing (expositions).
Look at the opening of **Terms for Dying**. The writer intends to engage the reader in an issue he thinks is important. Rhetorical questions can result in an exchange of ideas.

Great Fire of London

Detail of the Great Fire of London by an unknown painter, depicting the fire as it would have appeared on the evening of Tuesday, 4 Sept 1666 from a boat near Tower Wharf.

The Great Fire of London was a major fire that swept through the central parts of the city of London, from Sunday, 2 September to Wednesday, 5 September 1666. The fire gutted the medieval city inside the old Roman Wall. It threatened, but did not reach, the aristocratic district and most of the suburban slums. It consumed 13 200 houses, 87 parish churches, St Paul's Cathedral and most of the government buildings of the city. It is estimated to have destroyed the homes of 70 000 of the City's 80 000 inhabitants.

The death toll is unknown but thought to have been small, as only six verified deaths were recorded. This reasoning has recently been challenged on the grounds that the deaths of poor and middle-class people were not recorded. Sadly the heat of the fire may have cremated many victims leaving no recognisable remains.

The Great Fire started at the bakery of Thomas Farriner on Pudding Lane, shortly after midnight on Sunday, 2 September, and spread rapidly west across the City of London. The use of the major firefighting technique of the time, the creation of firebreaks by demolition was critically delayed because of the indecisiveness of the Lord Mayor. By the time large-scale demolitions were ordered on Sunday night, the wind had already fanned the bakery fire into a fire storm which defeated such measures.

a woodcut version of the fire

The fire pushed north on Monday into the heart of the City. Order in the streets broke down as rumours arose of suspicious foreigners setting fires. The fears of the homeless focused on the French and Dutch, England's enemies in an ongoing war. These immigrant groups became victims of lynching and street violence.

On Tuesday, the fire spread over most of the City, destroying St Paul's Cathedral and threatened Charles II's court. The battle to quench the fire is considered to have been won by two factors: the strong east winds died down, and the Tower of London garrison used gunpowder to create effective firebreaks to halt further spread eastward.

Despite numerous radical rebuilding proposals, London was reconstructed on essentially the same street plan used before the fire.

Sources: http://en.wikipedia.org/wiki/Great_Fire_of_London
http://www.newworldencyclopedia.org/entry/Great_Fire_of_London

Understanding Descriptions   Circle a letter or write an answer for questions 1 to 8.

1. Which part of London was destroyed in the *Great Fire*?
    A   the Roman Wall   B   the suburban slums
    C   the aristocratic district   D   a part of central London City

2. According to the text the greatest loss, because of the fire, was of
    A   churches   B   houses   C   slums   D   lives

3. What was the **main** method of containing major city fires in 1600s?
    A   quenching them with water   B   the controlled use of gunpowder
    C   creating firebreaks   D   waiting for a wind change

4. In which order did the events of the Great Fire occur?
    1. the fire turns north towards the city centre
    2. the Tower of London garrison creates a firebreak
    3. foreigners are blamed for the fire and lynched
    4. a bakery catches on fire
    A   4, 1, 3, 2   B   4, 3, 2, 1   C   1, 3, 2, 4   D   1, 4, 2, 3

5. Which factor, other than creating an effective firebreak, helped to contain the fire?
    Write your answer on the line. _____

6. Who could be considered most responsible for allowing the fire to spread?
    A   the baker in Pudding Lane   B   French and Dutch immigrants
    C   the Lord Mayor of London   D   the Tower of London garrison

7. Which word from the text means *destroyed*?
    A   consumed   B   firestorm   C   remains   D   cremated

8. In which of the following does the writer express an opinion?
    A   The Great Fire started at the bakery of Thomas Farriner
    B   the death toll is unknown but thought to have been small
    C   immigrant groups became victims of lynching and street violence
    D   sadly the heat of the fire may have cremated many victims

---

Lit Tip 8 – Improve your Literacy skills   **Tone in text**

Tone in writing is not really any different than the tone of your voice. You know that sometimes it is not *what* you say, but *how* you say it. Tone is the way the author expresses his attitude through his writing. The tone portrayed in the *Great Fire of London* is one of detachment.
Read the Practice passage again. Circle the word that best reflects the tone of this text.

factual   bitter   foreboding   sorrowful   despairing   nostalgic

Understanding Year 7 Comprehension
A. Horsfield © Five Senses Education © W. Marlin

9 Read the explanation *Elimination Tournaments.*

Elimination Tournaments

A single-elimination tournament — also called an Olympic system tournament, a knockout, single penetration, or sudden death tournament — is a type of elimination tournament where the loser of each match is immediately eliminated from winning the championship or first prize in the event. Only the right side of the diagram below would be used in a single - elimination tournament.

A double-elimination tournament is broken into two sets of brackets, generally called the winners' bracket and the losers' bracket. Each team/player begins in the winner's bracket, but with a loss in the first match the loser goes into a loser's bracket, where they have the opportunity to 'win' in the loser's bracket or consolation draw.

Draw for a double-elimination tournament

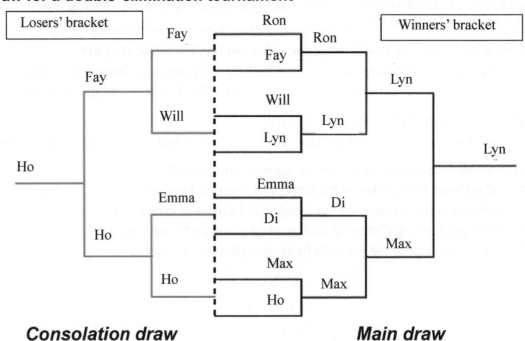

Consolation draw   *Main draw*

The black side (bracket) of the draw starts with four matches. It goes on to show the players who won their matches in each round and move on to play another game. After the first round all losers are eliminated from the winners' bracket.

From the above draw Ron played Fay and won. He went on to play Lyn.

Fay lost her first match but went on to play the loser of the match between Will and Lyn.

The red side (bracket) of the draw shows the players who lost their matches in the first round and moved on to play a game against another loser. If they lost they were out of the competition.

Sources: http://en.wikipedia.org/wiki/Single-elimination_tournament;squashclub.org

Understanding Explanations   Circle a letter or write an answer for questions 1 to 8.

1. What is another name for a single elimination tournament?
    A   a knock-out comp   B   a consolation draw
    C   a bracket event   D   a match competition

2. How many games did Fay play?

    Write your answer in the box. [   ]

3. Which of these players won the most games?
    A   Di   B   Ho   C   Will   D   Emma

4. In paragraph 2 the word *win* is in inverted commas.
    This is to indicate that
    A   the writer could not think of the correct word
    B   the word has greater importance than the word loss
    C   the writer is confused about what is happening
    D   the word is not used entirely correctly

5. As used in the text the word *bracket* means
    A   a mark to enclose text or numbers
    B   the structure of an elimination draw
    C   people who belong to a similar category
    D   a support for people in competitions

6. Who played the most winning games?

    Write your answer in the box. [   ]

7. What part of speech is the word *draw* as used in paragraph 3?
    A   noun   B   conjunction   C   preposition   D   verb

8. According to the text which statement is TRUE?
    A   The winners of both brackets are of equal status.
    B   The consolation draw is more important than the main draw.
    C   In a single elimination tournament losers get a second chance to win.
    D   Everyone plays at least two games in a double elimination tournament.

Lit Tip 9 – Improve your Literacy skills   The suffix ee

A **suffix** is a group of letters (morpheme) added to the end of a word to modify its meaning. Double e (ee) is a suffix often used to refer to a person being something.
An *absentee* is an absent person; a trainee is a person in training.
What do you call a person who:

escapes _____, is divorced _____, is deported _____

is employed _____, is addressed _____, is invited _____
Of course, all words that end with ee do not refer to people.
Examples: goatee (a beard), jubilee (an anniversary), coffee (a drink), frisbee (a toy)

Understanding Year 7 Comprehension
A. Horsfield © Five Senses Education © W. Marlin

Pigeon Houses of France

Pigeon houses in France come in many shapes and styles. Here are two different pigeon houses.

A pigeon house or dovecote is a structure intended to house pigeons or doves. It may be square or circular, a free-standing structure or built onto the end of a house or barn. It generally contained pigeonholes for the birds to nest. Pigeons and doves were an important food source historically in France and were kept for their eggs, flesh, and dung. Pigeons produce valuable fertilizer, considered superior for agricultural purposes to poultry waste.

However when crops were being sown farmers had to close the pigeon house to stop the birds from eating the seeds.

The possession of a dovecote was a symbol of status and power for the nobles and clergy and was consequently regulated by laws of the period - that was before the French Revolution (1788). After that, they became an important adjunct to any self-respecting farmhouse, signifying the end of feudal rights.

Towards the end of the 17th century, France had nearly 42 000 pigeon-houses, mostly in the south where the right to rearing pigeons was not always a privilege of the feudal lord.

The dovecote interior, the space inside for the pigeons, was divided into a number of boulins (pigeonholes). Each

Photo: A. Horsfield

boulin provided lodgings for a pair of pigeons. Some pigeon houses contained over 1 000 pigeons.

There were a few common sense safety rules to be followed. Pigeon houses were built sheltered from prevailing winds and away from large trees to keep birds of prey at bay. If possible they were built on a higher part of the land to provide ease of access.

Smooth walls and a row of varnished tiles were designed to stop rodents and other predators from getting in. If the pigeon house had two storeys, only the second floor was used for the pigeons.

The 19th century saw the loss of importance of the pigeons as agricultural techniques were perfected and chemical fertilisers were adopted.

Sources: http://en.wikipedia.org/wiki/Dovecote,
http://suriyakantha.chez.com/Pigeons.htm
Tour map: La route des pigeonniers Tarn Tourism

Understanding Reports

Circle a letter or write an answer for questions 1 to 8.

1. A pigeon house is much the same thing as a dovecote.

   Is this TRUE or FALSE? Tick a box.   TRUE ☐   FALSE ☐

2. To deter predators from entering pigeon houses French farmers
   - A   attached them to their homes
   - B   built them under large trees
   - C   sited them on high land
   - D   tiled the access points

3. Which of the following statements is based on evidence in the passage?
   - A   Pigeon ownership was a recreational pursuit for the well-to-do.
   - B   Owning pigeons was once considered a symbol of social importance.
   - C   The nobles had a preference for poultry rather than pigeons.
   - D   The French Revolution was a result of discriminatory pigeon laws.

4. Pigeons were **NOT** kept by French farmers to
   - A   provide meat
   - B   produce eggs
   - C   deliver messages
   - D   supply manure

5. The word *adjunct* in paragraph 4 refers to
   - A   an additional, useful facility
   - B   the cover for a pigeon house
   - C   a point where things meet
   - D   a second entrance for pigeons

6. Why did pigeon houses lose their importance in France?
   - A   the influence of the clergy and nobles diminished
   - B   there was a lessening reliance on pigeon products in agriculture
   - C   the feudal lords had a decreasing control of the use of land
   - D   the number of pigeons decreased after the French Revolution

7. The term *waste* as used in paragraph 1, is a euphemism for
   (Check **Lit Tip 6** for assistance.)
   - A   remains
   - B   scraps
   - C   manure
   - D   rubbish

8. Why did southern France have more pigeon houses than other parts of France?
   - A   there was a greater variety of pigeons in southern France
   - B   farmland required a greater amount of natural fertilisers
   - C   there were more feudal properties in southern France
   - D   owning pigeons wasn't restricted to the nobles and clergy

---

Lit Tip 10 – Improve your Literacy skills   Dashes

The dash (-) is a form of punctuation. It has several functions.
1. The dash can be used to indicate an interruption in something being said.
Example 1: Mum began to say, "Before you leave this - " when her phone jangled.
Example 2: Jean said, "The pen was taken by - "
   "Don't say who!" quickly interrupted the teacher.
2. A dash can be used to substitute for namely or a similar expression.
There was just one culprit - Jacko.
3. A dash can be used to create emphasis.
To feed the victims - that is a real achievement.
Remember: hyphens are used to connect words: two-fifteen, north-west, non-fiction

Understanding Year 7 Comprehension
A. Horsfield © Five Senses Education © W. Marlin

The Tidy Towns Scheme

No one had been interested in Rudi until he began speaking loudly in the council reception area about doggie poops on the street. He didn't actually say 'poops'.

He finally got to see the Health Officer, Ms Rees. Her office was covered in Tidy Towns competition posters. She wanted success for Sandbar.

When Rudi complained about the dog droppings on the footpath Ms Rees ruefully rubbed her chin. It was an on-going problem she admitted. Then an idea. It would make Sandbar's Tidy Town competition entry look unique if some citizen 'volunteered' to be a poop ranger until Clean-Up Australia Day. Both the Tidy Towns competition and Clean Up Australia were worthwhile community projects, she had explained excitedly.

Rudi had frowned. He was on a different page. 'Council can only do so much. People might be shamed into doing the right thing,' reasoned Ms Rees. She looked at Rudi. 'What about you?' Rudi was dumbstruck. How about a big a fat NO for starters!

'The high school is participating – Tidy Town's a community effort. You could help your school and community. What about it?' Rudi wasn't thrilled with the suggestion. In fact, he was mortified.

'We'll make it a big thing with an article in the Council Newsletter. With your photo. You might make Student of the Week.'

'Never happen,' growled Rudi. 'No good at sport – or schoolwork! Anyhow, Mitch Smith has his name permanently engraved on that.'

'You'd be a legend!' Ms Rees purred.

Wheels started to turn in Rudi's brain - slowly, but they had begun to move.

Ms Rees looked at him expectantly, head to one side.

'Tidy Towns stories are reported on TV,' Ms Rees had said. I bet her eyebrows raised and she had been smiling. It's an old trick!

Rudi finally capitulated and accepted the challenge. Mum and Dad had to give permission and then Ms Rees organised for a hi-vis orange vest emblazoned with the Sandbar crest. That made Rudi feel important. Me? I was flabbergasted!

On Thursday Ms Rees came to our place. Beaming, she gave Rudi a bundle of small, black plastic bags and demonstrated how to pick it up! I didn't watch, even though she used a plastic turd for the demonstration.

'Well?' she said with an inquiring smile and raised eyebrows.

'No worries,' grinned Rudi. Me? I think my bottom jaw dropped off!

Understanding Narratives   Circle a letter or write an answer for questions 1 to 8.

1. What was upsetting Rudi the most?
    - A   Mitch Smith always getting the Student of the Week award
    - B   dog droppings in public places
    - C   his school being involved in the Tidy Towns Award
    - D   the suggestion made by Ms Rees

2. To encourage Rudi to participate in the cleaning up of doggie droppings Ms Rees
    - A   offered him a Student of the Week award
    - B   supplied an orange vest emblazoned with the Sandbar crest
    - C   enticed Rudi with the chance of some recognition in the media
    - D   provided a free demonstration on how to collect doggie droppings

3. What does the narrator mean when he states Rudi *was on a different page*?
    - A   Rudi was not having the same thoughts as Ms Rees
    - B   Rudi was anticipating what Ms Rees had in mind
    - C   Rudi was looking at the posters on the office wall
    - D   Rudi was getting himself into a difficult situation

4. When the narrator understood what Ms Rees was suggesting he had feelings of
    - A   weariness   B   excitement   C   pride   D   disbelief

5. As used in the text, what does the word *hi-vis* stand for?
    Write your answer on the line. _____

6. How did Rudi's attitude change over the time he spent in Ms Rees's office?
    - A   from anger to suspicion
    - B   from frustration to ambition
    - C   from despair to hope
    - D   from disbelief to willingness

7. What person is the last sentence written in?
    - A   first person   B   second person   C   third person

8. A suitable alternative title for the extract would be
    - A   Sandbar's problem   B   Ms Rees's ambition
    - C   Getting heard   D   Rudi is hoodwinked!

Lit Tip 11 – Improve your Literacy skills   Portmanteau words

Did you have any difficulties with question 5? Read on.
A portmanteau word is a word that is created by blending the parts of two words to create a new word,
e.g. *motel* comes from <u>mot</u>or and h<u>otel</u>, *blog* from we<u>b</u> and <u>log</u>,
brunch: <u>br</u>eakfast/<u>lunch</u>, skyjack: <u>sky</u>/hi<u>jack</u>, guesstimate: <u>guess</u>/es<u>timate</u>
Which two words are used to form these words? (You may use reference resources.)

smog: _____/_____ , **ginormous:** _____/_____

liger: _____/_____ , **email:** _____/_____

skype: _____/_____ ,**chortle:** _____/_____

Understanding Year 7 Comprehension
A. Horsfield © Five Senses Education © W. Marlin

12 Read the Book review of *Kangaroo* by John Simons.

Book Review-Kangaroo

Reviewed by Jill Mather

This book is part of the 'Animals' series and contributes a comprehensive account of the well-loved macropods. The text is, as expected, extensive in its coverage from the mythical to the factual. This study delves into the little known features as well as the lighter side of the admired animal. Perhaps we can thank the famous television series Skippy, the Bush Kangaroo for popularising this iconic animal. There is little doubt that the kangaroo has become a symbol of Australia.

John Simons introduces his work by asking the question - What is a kangaroo? He explores the strangeness of this animal and its portrayal as a rather frightening creature hopping down a deserted street, enveloped in a fading light, as used in another television series.

Simons moves to a more positive aspect of this much-loved marsupial. Its biological strangeness is fully explained; its amazing adaptability to climatic conditions; preferred habitat; its connection with the spreading of human and urban___(4)_____.

Exploring various types of genus Macropus takes the reader into a highly detailed and informative section on the variety of animals, from the large Reds and Greys to the very small. It's a diverse and interesting compilation.

The interaction of the Kangaroo and Indigenous people was inevitable. As a food source it was important. Simons goes on to provide the reader with a plethora of fascinating information which includes the use of the kangaroo in cartoons, children's literature, film and stories.

As a reference guide it makes an important contribution to a subject of which most of us know something, but certainly not all. It is valuable as a reference guide. The many colour plates aid the recognition of the various species. The narrative is assembled in a logical progression which takes in the animals at home and abroad in an enjoyable and very informative manner. This book is ideal for students and those with a desire to know more about this iconic animal.

Jill Mather is the author of five non-fiction books.

(Kangaroo was published in 2012.)

My thanks to Jill Mather for permission to reproduce this review.

From: Newsbite The NSW Writers' Centre Monday 18 March 2013.

Understanding Reviews

Circle a letter or write an answer for questions 1 to 8.

1. The book, *Kangaroo*, could best be described as a
   - A picture book
   - B manual
   - C reference book
   - D catalogue

2. According to the review which statement about *Kangaroo* is CORRECT?
   - A *Kangaroo* is the first book written by Simons.
   - B *Kangaroo* is the only non-fiction work by Simons.
   - C *Kangaroo* is an out-of-print book written by Simons.
   - D *Kangaroo* is one of a number of related books by Simons.

3. The reviewer twice refers to the kangaroo as being *iconic*.
   By *iconic* she means the kangaroo
   - A is an endangered species
   - B symbolises Australia
   - C is one of many macropods
   - D needs protection

4. A word has been deleted from the text.
   Which word would be best suited to the space (4)?
   - A destruction
   - B pollution
   - C settlement
   - D ignorance

5. The reviewer finds the greatest value of *Kangaroo* is the way in which
   - A it includes a wide range of original information
   - B the text portrays the importance of kangaroos to Indigenous Australians
   - C a variety of threats to macropods are clearly described in the text
   - D it exposes how television made the kangaroo a national symbol

6. Which two macropod species does Mather specifically mention in her review?
   Write your answer on the line. _____ and _____

7. Jill Mather's review of Kangaroo could best be described as
   - A positive
   - B hesitant
   - C extravagant
   - D unkind

8. According to the reviewer which group is most likely to find this book useful?
   - A Indigenous Australians
   - B producers of television series
   - C Australians living overseas
   - D those involved in macropod research

Lit Tip 12 – Improve your Literacy skills   Short word origins

English is an ever-changing language.
English words are often shortened or abbreviated. This may seem like bad English at first but often, over time, the shortened word may become accepted.
Look at how these words have changed.
perambulator - pram, utility - ute, bicycle - bike, gymnasium - gym, aeroplane - plane
Find the original word for these common short words. (You may use reference material.)
fridge _____, zoo _____, taxi _____
bus _____, app _____, van _____

Understanding Year 7 Comprehension
A. Horsfield © Five Senses Education © W. Marlin

Meanings Change

Do you ever stop to think about the words awesome and awful? The original meaning of awe was a feeling of fear or wonder or dread. But awful and awesome are so overused that the original meaning of the words has been watered down considerably. Now if something is described as awesome it usually implies something is pretty good or cool.

In the year 1666 a great fire swept through London and destroyed more than half the city, including three-quarters of St. Paul's Cathedral. Sir Christopher Wren, the original designer of the cathedral, and perhaps the finest architect of all time, was commissioned to rebuild the great edifice. He began in 1675 and finished in 1710 - a remarkably short time for such a task. When the magnificent edifice was completed, Queen Anne, the reigning monarch, visited the cathedral and told Wren that his work was "awful, artificial, and amusing." Sir Christopher, so the story goes, was delighted with the royal compliment, because in those days awful meant "full of awe - awe-inspiring", artificial meant "artistic," and amusing, from the muses, meant "amazing."

That was over 300 years ago. Today, the older, flattering meanings of awful, artificial, and amusing have virtually disappeared from popular use. Indeed, the general rule of language is that when a single word develops two polar meanings, one will become obsolete. Occasionally, though, two diametrically opposed meanings of the same English word survive, and the technical term for these same-words-opposite meanings pairs is contronyms. More popularly, they are known as Janus words because the Roman god Janus had two faces that looked in opposite directions.

Here's a little finger exercise. Remember that I'm the teacher, so you must try to do what I ask. You should be able to follow this. Make a circle with the fingers on your left hand by touching the tip of your index finger to the tip of your thumb. Now poke your head through that circle.

If you unsuccessfully tried to fit your head through the small digital circle, you (and almost any reader) thought that the phrase "poke your head" meant that your head was the poker. But if you raised your left hand with the circle of fingers up close to your forehead and poked your right index finger through that circle until it touched your forehead, you realized that the phrase "poke your head" has a second, and opposite, meaning: that the head is the 'pokee'. (Check out Lit Tip 9.)

Source: http://learningenglish.voanews.com/content/a-23-2009-11-03-voa1-83142707/117546.html

Understanding Reports

Circle a letter or write an answer for questions 1 to 8.

1. According to the text, the 17th century (the 1600s) meaning of amusing meant
   - A   entertaining
   - B   amazing
   - C   funny
   - D   clever

2. The text *Meanings Change* is most likely intended to be
   - A   confusing
   - B   hilarious
   - C   informative
   - D   provocative

3. In which year did Sir Christopher Wren finish the rebuilding of St Paul's Cathedral?

   Write your answer in the box. ☐

4. Which line from the text expresses an opinion?
   - A   You should be able to follow this.
   - B   That was over 300 years ago.
   - C   The originally meaning of awe was a feeling of fear or wonder or dread.
   - D   Now poke your head through that circle.

5. The main purpose of the finger exercise in paragraph 4 is to
   - A   test the reader's ability to follow directions
   - B   provide the reader with an amusing manipulative exercise
   - C   explain why Sir Christopher Wren misunderstood the queen's comment
   - D   demonstrate how words can have conflicting meanings

6. The word *pokee* (last paragraph) is meant to show that (Check out **Lit Tip 9**.)
   - A   there was a 17th century word for being poked at
   - B   the writer couldn't think of a suitable word
   - C   the head is the recipient of the poker's poke (finger)
   - D   any attempt to follow the directions was foolish

7. Which word with a similar meaning could replace *polar* (par. 3) as used in the text?
   - A   popular
   - B   different
   - C   frigid
   - D   opposite

8. The writer's tone could be described as (Check out **Lit Tip 8**.)
   - A   cheerful
   - B   demanding
   - C   brash
   - D   sarcastic

Lit Tip 13 – Improve your Literacy skills   **Singular verbs**

We think of singular nouns **without** the s suffix.
Singular verbs appear to contradict this pattern. Singular **regular** verbs take an s!
The plural s on the end of nouns has **nothing** to do with the s on the end of verbs.
A singular subject (noun) needs a singular verb: The boy (subject) swims in the river.
A plural subject (noun) needs a plural verb: The boys (subject) swim in the river.
Sometimes the subject is not near the verb. The can of baked beans sits on the table.
Underline the correct verb in these.

1. The cat (chase / chases) mice.   2. A herd of cows (graze / grazes) near the dam.

3. The gang (fire / fires) several shots.   4. Dad (see / sees) all my mistakes.

Understanding Year 7 Comprehension
A. Horsfield © Five Senses Education © W. Marlin

14 Read the poem *The Brook* by Alfred, Lord Tennyson.

The Brook

I come from haunts of coot* and hern*,
I make a sudden sally
And sparkle out among the fern,
To bicker down a valley.

By thirty hills I hurry down,
Or slip between the ridges,
By twenty thorpes², a little town,
And half a hundred bridges.

Till last by Philip's farm I flow
To join the brimming river,
For men may come and men may go,
But I go on forever.

I chatter over stony ways,
In little sharps and trebles,
I bubble into eddying bays,
I babble on the pebbles.

With many a curve my banks I fret
By many a field and fallow³,
And many a fairy foreland set
With willow-weed⁴ and mallow⁴.

I chatter, chatter, as I flow
To join the brimming river,
For men may come and men may go,
But I go on forever.

I slip, I slide, I gloom, I glance,
Among my skimming swallows;
I make the netted sunbeam dance
Against my sandy shallows.

I murmur under moon and stars
In brambly wildernesses;
I linger by my shingly bars;
I loiter round my cresses;

*	water birds
2	villages
3	unplanted field
4	river weeds

And out again I curve and flow
To join the brimming river,
For men may come and men may go,

But I go on forever.

Alfred, Lord Tennyson (1809 - 1892)

Understanding Poetry   Circle a letter to answer questions 1 to 8.

1. The narrator of the poem is
   - A   the brook
   - B   Philip, the farmer
   - C   a rower
   - D   a villager

2. Once the brook has passed by towns and bridges it next
   - A   sparkles out among the fern
   - B   passes by Philip's farm
   - C   joins the brimming river
   - D   makes a sudden sally

3. The poet uses the word *netted* (stanza 7) to emphasise the
   - A   patterns in shallow water made by shimmering rays of light
   - B   trapping of river fish in shallow water
   - C   tangle of brambly wildernesses
   - D   network of brooks and rivers of the countryside

4. What is the underlying issue in the poem, *The Brook*?
   - A   brooks can pass through many different places
   - B   there is a similarity between nature and people
   - C   unlike nature the time on earth for humans is limited
   - D   there is little in life that is predictable

5. Look at the lines: *I slip, I slide, I gloom, I glance;*
                              I murmur under moon and stars.
   The sounds of the words in these lines suggest that the brook is (Check out Lit Tip 14)
   - A   gushing along
   - B   trickling by
   - C   smashing into obstacles
   - D   flowing quietly

6. Which stanza alludes to musical sounds?
   - A   stanza 1   B   stanza 4   C   stanza 7   D   stanza 8

7. To capture a feature of the brook Tennyson has relied mainly upon words portraying
   - A   countryside smells
   - B   emotional images
   - C   touch sensations
   - D   a variety of sounds

8. The imagery in the poem suggests the journey of the brook is one from
   - A   daring to confidence
   - B   calmness to excitement
   - C   liveliness to tranquillity
   - D   danger to security

Lit Tip 14 – Improve your Literacy skills   Assonance in poetry

Assonance is the repetition of a particular Sounds in words to create an effect. It occurs when vowels are repeated in words that are close together, usually in poetry. It enhances the meaning within the words, e.g. the monotonous drone of sombre songs.
Which line from Stanza 6 has the best example of assonance? Write it on the line.

_____

(**Note:** Consonance is the repetition of important consonant sounds in a line.)

Playing Dominoes

A domino is a small tile that is commonly called a bone. It is rectangular with a line down the centre. Each end of the tile contains a number. The numbers vary from 0 (or blank) to 6. This produces 28 unique tiles.

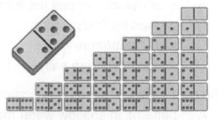

A common domino size is about 3 cm long, 1.5 cm wide, and 0.5 cm thick - small enough to be held comfortably in the hand, but large enough to be easily manipulated, and thick enough to stand on its edge.

Dominoes are referred to by the number of dots (or pips) on each end, with the lower number usually listed first. A tile with a 2 on one end and a 5 on the other is referred to as a "2-5". A tile with the same number on both ends is called a "double". A "6-6" is referred to as "double-six". A double-six is the "heaviest" domino; a double-blank is the "lightest" domino value.

Tiles which have ends with the same number of pips are members of the same "suit". There are seven suits.

There are many games to be played with dominoes. This one is for 2 to 4 players.

1. Place the tiles facedown on the table and shuffle them until they are random. This pile is called the bone yard.

Typical dominoes game in progress

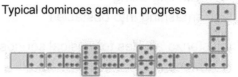

2. Each player takes seven dominoes from the bone yard. These are stood on their edge facing the player thereby keeping their value secret.

3. The player with the highest double goes first. The player places that domino face up on the table. Play is in a clockwise direction.

4. The next player places a domino with like value next to the first domino (either end is okay).

5. Players pick from the bone yard (if less than four players) if they don't have a domino that corresponds to the ones on the layout. Dominoes are kept concealed from opponent(s).

6. A player passes if that player is unable to go.

7. The winner is the first person to run out of tiles. However if everybody passes, the winner is the person with the lowest score. The score is determined by the dots remaining in the player's tiles.

Dominoes usually come in a box.

8. Games may be repeated until a player has an accumulation of 50 points. At this point the player with the least points wins.

Sources: http://www.ehow.com/how_9241_play-dominoes.html
http://www.domino-games.com/domino-rules/draw-dominoes-rules.html

Understanding Procedures

Circle a letter to answer questions 1 to 8.

1. How many dominoes come in a set of boxed dominoes?
   - A   14
   - B   24
   - C   28
   - D   36

2. What is in the bone yard of a dominoes game?
   - A   any tiles that are face up in the game
   - B   the tiles each player has standing on their edges
   - C   any tile that a player cannot place in the game in progress
   - D   all face-down unplayed tiles in the pool of unchosen tiles

3. How are domino tiles named?
   - A   by the number of pips on each end - lowest number first
   - B   by the total number of pips on the tile
   - C   by the suit in which they occur
   - D   by their proximity to any double tile

4. No player has a double six to begin a particular game.
   The player most likely to start the play will have
   - A   a tile with a blank end
   - B   the next highest double
   - C   a tile with the least number of pips
   - D   a 5-6 tile

5. A double tile is usually placed
   - A   next to another double tile
   - B   beside a tile with a lower pip count
   - C   at right angles to the preceding tile
   - D   at the corner of the tiles in play

6. If at the end of a game all players pass, the winner will be the player with the
   - A   least number of tiles
   - B   highest total of tile dots
   - C   highest 'double' tile
   - D   least number of tile dots

7. Which word is a synonym for *manipulated* as used in paragraph 2?
   - A   controlled
   - B   managed
   - C   operated
   - D   manoeuvred

8. What is the maximum number of players a standard box of dominoes is suitable for?
   - A   four
   - B   six
   - C   seven
   - D   eight

Lit Tip 15 – Improve your Literacy skills   **Regular verbs / irregular verbs**

Regular verbs change their form very little when used in a variety of situations.
The past tense usually ends with the addition of *ed*: work/worked, carry/carried
Regular verbs tend to follow the same pattern or rules when adding suffixes.
Irregular verbs have their own set of 'rules'. The past tense of *speak* is *spoke*.
Look at these: have/had, drink/drank, bet/bet, bite/bit, break/broke, say/said, meet/met
Underline the irregular verbs: ride   clean   write   pay   wreck   trip   say   send
Write the past tense for these irregular verbs.

sell _____, throw _____, win _____, bring _____, leave _____

Understanding Year 7 Comprehension
A. Horsfield © Five Senses Education © W. Marlin

Pulp Magazines

Pulp magazines were inexpensive fiction magazines that were published from 1896 through to the late 1950s. The term pulp derives from the cheap wood pulp paper on which the magazines were printed.

Before the superhero comics of the Golden Age (1930s, 1940s), pulp magazines featured heroic stories and are considered the predecessors to superhero comic books.

The introduction of the comic book format came in 1933 with the publication of Famous Funnies. A graphic novel (popular since the 1970s) is a publication made up of 'comic' content for more mature readers.

Sources: http://www.teara.govt.nz/en/comics-and-graphic-novels/page-http://en.wikipedia.org/wiki/Comic_book

Understanding Persuasions

Circle a letter to answer questions 1 to 8.

1. From the cover illustrations, the genre of these stories would best be described as
   - A   mystery stories
   - B   action stories
   - C   historical stories
   - D   fantasy stories

2. The magazines have been numbered.
   From the cover graphic which magazine is least likely to have a science fiction story?
   - A   **1** *Tom Corbett, Space Cadet*
   - B   **2** *Amazing Stories: Paul Revere and the Time Machine*
   - C   **3** *Atomic War*
   - D   **4** *Amazing Stories (by various authors)*

3. The cost of these examples of pulp fiction ranged between 10c and 25c.
   This apparent low price is a reflection of the
   - A   poor quality of the paper
   - B   cost of publication over fifty year ago
   - C   inferior storylines
   - D   inexperience of the writers

4. The word *comic* in the last sentence is in inverted commas. (Check out **Lit Tip 15**)
   This is done to indicate that the word
   - A   has been taken out of context
   - B   is a misspelled word
   - C   is a bold exaggeration
   - D   needs its meaning clarified

5. The magazines are described as *pulp fiction* because
   - A   the stories are not well written
   - B   the magazine presentation is showy
   - C   they appeal to a less educated reading group
   - D   they are printed on cheap quality paper

6. Tom Corbett is described as a *Space Cadet* (magazine 1). Corbett is most likely a
   - A   commander of a spaceship
   - B   deputy law-enforcer
   - C   young trainee in an armed service
   - D   person engaged to carry items

7. Which word would best describe the tone in *Atomic War* (3)? (See **Lit Tip 8**.)
   - A   patriotic
   - B   informative
   - C   persuasive
   - D   factual

8. Superhero comics emerged as a popular form of reading
   - A   before pulp fiction
   - B   before *Famous Funnies*
   - C   after graphic novels
   - D   after pulp fiction

Lit Tip 16 – Improve your Literacy skills   **Inverted commas**

Inverted commas do more than enclose direct speech (actual words spoken).
They can be used to:
- clarify meaning: I can never remember how to spell 'alcohol'.
- show that the words are not the original words of the writer:
  Dad has his opinion on how to 'stop the boats'.
- indicate that a word has been used out of its original meaning:
  The rabbits had 'craters' all over the paddock!

Add inverted commas to the appropriate words in these sentences.
1. I had a visit from my friend, the debt collector.
2. Matt was looking for assistance in the dictionary.

Understanding Year 7 Comprehension
A. Horsfield © Five Senses Education © W. Marlin

Read the recount *Lake Taupo.*

Lake Taupo

Lake Taupo is the largest lake by surface area in New Zealand.

Lake Facts

Lake Taupo Photo: A. Horsfield

Lake Taupo (originally Taupomoana) has an area of 616 sq km, is 40 kilometres long and 27 kilometres across at the widest part. The greatest depth is 159 metres and the surface of the lake is 359 metres above sea level. The length length of shoreline is 193 kilometres. The lake is fed by many streams. Water leaves the lake via the Waikato River outlet.

Geological Origins

Lake Taupo lies in a caldera created by a supervolcanic eruption which occurred approximately 27 000 years ago. According to geological records, the volcano has erupted 28 times in the last 27 000 years.

Early map of Lake Taupo

The initial event, 27 000 years ago is known as the Oruanui eruption. It was the world's largest known eruption over the past 70 000 years, ejecting altogether 1 170 cubic kilometres of material and causing several hundred square kilometres of surrounding land to collapse and form the caldera. The last recorded eruption was around 1310 A.D.

The Legend of the Origin of Lake Taupo

When Maoris from the Arafura first came and landed at Maketu, the chief, Tohunga Ngatoro, took a party inland, arriving at the summit of Tauhara.

From there he saw a new land with a large barren basin. To improve the waste area with afforestation he plucked a large Tatora tree branch and threw it into the basin. The wind caused him to miss his mark, and striking a bank at the edge of the basin, it bounced, and landed upside down. The branches pierced the ground, water gushed up and Lake Taupo was formed.

Even today the tree can be seen about 60 metres off shore at Wharewaka. The tree is called a Pere (the arrow of) Ngatoro.

When Ngatoro came down from Tauhora and saw the lake he had created he held a thanksgiving service. He decided to stock the lake with eels and so plucked a tassel from the mat he was wearing and threw it into the water. It turned into an eel and wriggled away. But____(6)____and to this day no eels can be found in Lake Taupo.

Sources: http://en.wikipedia.org/wiki/Lake_Taupo
http://www.taupodc.govt.nz/our-district/about-our-district/history/Pages/history.aspx
http://gonewzealand.about.com/od/Rotorua-Lake-Taupo-Destination/a/Lake-Taupo-Facts-And-Figures.htm

Understanding Recounts

Circle a letter or write an answer for questions 1 to 8.

1. Where is Lake Taupo located?
   A   by the Maori landing site at Maketu
   B   near Arafura
   C   at the mouth of the Waikato River
   D   in the crater of a volcano

2. What is the distance around Lake Taupo?
   A   27 km   B   40 km   C   67 km   D   193 km

3. Tick a box for the CORRECT fact.   1. Lake Tapo is a saltwater lake.   ☐

                                             2. Lake Taupo is a fresh water lake. ☐

4. Which point from the legend of the origin of *Lake Taupo* is most likely CORRECT?
   A   the tassel from Ngatoro's mat turned into an eel
   B   a branch pierced the land and released water into the lake
   C   there are no eels in Lake Taupo
   D   Lake Taupo was a dry basin when the Maoris arrived

5. Which fact from the text about Lake Taupo is CORRECT?
   A   Lake Taupo is situated at sea level.
   B   Lake Taupo is longer than it is wide.
   C   Lake Taupo was formed in 1310 A.D.
   D   Lake Taupo is sinking into the volcano.

6. Words have been deleted from the text.
   Which words would be best suited to the space (6)?
   A   it soon died
   B   Ngatoro found another stick
   C   the volcano erupted
   D   the lake dried up

7. The opening sentence states:
   Lake Taupo is the largest lake by surface area in New Zealand.
   This suggests that
   A   the size of other lakes is fully documented
   B   Lake Taupo has conditions that keep changing
   C   Lake Taupo contains less water than some other lakes
   D   surface area is not a logical way to compare lakes

8. The word basin as used in the text refers to a
   A   cooking receptacle
   B   depression in the landform
   C   water-filled valley
   D   storage container

Lit Tip 17 – Improve your Literacy skills   What is irony?

Irony is a figure of speech where there is a gap between what is said and what is meant. The usual meaning of the word is more or less opposite to what is intended.
Irony is often intended to amuse and not intended to be vindictive - unlike sarcasm.
Examples: 1. You may compliment a tennis opponent on a *fine* shot when his return shot goes over the tennis court fence!
2. The name of Britain's largest dog is 'Tiny'.
3. I posted a video on YouTube about how useless YouTube is.

Understanding Year 7 Comprehension
A. Horsfield © Five Senses Education © W. Marlin

White Island Visit

Leaving the harbour on our way to White Island we passed the bronze statue of Wairaka, daughter of the great navigator Toroa.

White Island is about 50km off the coast. It is New Zealand's most accessible volcano. On arrival at the island we were <u>tendered</u> ashore to a rocky point. Here we put on protective clothing and carried gas masks for times when the smell of sulphur fumes became overpowering.

We were in a small, guided group for safety. We got close to the steaming crater and walked by boiling pools of mud.

White Island (Whakari) is an active cone volcano which has been built up by continuous volcanic activity over the past 150,000 years. About 70 percent of the volcano is under the sea. It is the largest volcanic structure in New Zealand.

Water in the streams runs hot.

White Island was in eruption from Dec 1975 to Sept 2000, the longest historic eruption episode.

Photos: A. Horsfield

A sulphur-mining venture began in 1885. This was stopped abruptly in 1914 when part of the crater wall collapsed and a landslide destroyed the sulphur mine and miners' village. Twelve lives were lost. The remains of the slowly corroding equipment were the last things we saw as we left - but the smell lingered on.

Understanding Recounts

Circle a letter to answer questions 1 to 8.

1. As a geological feature what makes White Island volcano important?
   - A   It is New Zealand's only volcano.
   - B   The volcano was a source of sulphur.
   - C   It is an active volcano whose bulk is below sea level.
   - D   The volcano was the cause of the death of twelve miners.

2. What caused the close-down of the sulphur mining venture on White Island?
   - A   depletion of sulphur supplies
   - B   living conditions became unbearable
   - C   the volcano erupted
   - D   deaths caused by a landslide

3. The last thing the visitors experienced as they departed the island was the
   - A   smell of sulphur
   - B   sight of corroding machinery
   - C   heat from the mud ponds
   - D   volcano erupting

4. In which order did the visitors do the following when visiting White Island?
   - 1   The group make their way to volcano's crater.
   - 2   The tour boat passes by the bronze statue of Wairaka.
   - 3   Visitors to the volcano are ferried to the island.
   - 4   White Island visitors put on protective gear.
   - A   4, 2, 1, 3
   - B   1, 2, 3, 4
   - C   2, 3, 4, 1
   - D   2, 4, 3, 1

5. According to the text when was the last volcanic eruption on White Island?
   - A   1885
   - B   1914
   - C   1975
   - D   2000

6. What was the weather like on the day the tour group went to White Island?
   - A   windy
   - B   misty
   - C   overcast
   - D   bright

7. As used in the recount, what does tendered mean?
   - A   cared for
   - B   transported
   - C   made a bid
   - D   softened

8. According to the text which fact is CORRECT?
   - A   White Island is 50 km from the New Zealand mainland.
   - B   White Island hasn't erupted in 150 000 years.
   - C   Mining on the island commenced in 1914.
   - D   The volcano erupts every 75 years.

Lit Tip 18 – Improve your Literacy skills   **Brackets (a style of parenthesis)**

Round brackets are a form of punctuation. They are used to enclose extra information that the writer feels is required to make meaning clearer. In many ways they are short cuts to providing additional information.

Examples: 1. Sue Ling (1983 - 2013) had a short but full life. The dates in brackets indicate when Sue lived.

2. Brackets can enclose scientific names for plants and animal - usually in italics.

3. Brackets can provide initials for organizations which are referred to later in the text.

Removing the words in brackets does not change the sense the sentence makes.

Add brackets to this sentence.

The work of the Sydney City Council SCC will interrupt peak-hour traffic.

Understanding Year 7 Comprehension
A. Horsfield © Five Senses Education © W. Marlin

19 Read the biography **Bugs Bunny.**

Bugs Bunny

Since 1939, Bugs has starred in more than 175 films.
Every year from 1945 to 1961 he was voted "top animated character" by movie theatre owners when cartoons were still shown in cinemas.
For almost 30 years, starting in 1960, he had one of the top-rated shows on Saturday morning TV.

TIMELINE

1937: Warner Bros animation director Tex Avery makes *Porky's Duck Hunt*. Porky Pig hunted a screwball duck named Daffy who didn't get scared and run away when somebody pointed a gun at him, but leapt about like a maniac. When it hit the theatres, recalls a director, it was like an explosion.

1938: Warner Bros director Ben Hardaway remakes the cartoon with a rabbit instead of a duck, as *Porky's Hare Hunt*. One of Bugs' creators said that the rabbit was just Daffy Duck in a rabbit suit!

1939: Hardaway decides to remake *Porky's Hare Hunt* with a new rabbit (as Hare-um Scare-um). Cartoonist Charlie Thorson comes up with a grey and white rabbit with large buckteeth. He labels his sketch "Bugs' Bunny".

1940: Director Tex Avery becomes the real father of Bugs Bunny with *A Wild Hare*. Bugs is changed from a foolish lunatic to a street-smart, wise-alec. Bugs's debut as a star was the 1940 short *A Wild Hare*, when he first uttered his trademark line, "What's up Doc?" He was facing a gun and audiences expected the rabbit to scream, not make a casual remark. It got such a laugh that animators said, 'Let's use that every chance we get.' It made his character, Bugs was in command in the face of any danger." Bugs also got his voice in A Wild Hare. Mel Blanc, who did most Looney Tunes voices, had been having a hard time finding a voice for the rabbit. When Blanc was shown the latest rabbit sketch for *A Wild Hare* he wrote:

His posture had improved, he'd shed some weight, and his protruding front teeth weren't as pronounced. The most significant change, however, was in his facial expression. No longer just goofy, he was a sly looking rascal.

1958: Bugs wins his first Oscar after three nominations for *Knighty Knight, Bugs*.

1976: Americans voted on their favourite characters, real and imaginary. Bugs came in second.

1985: Bugs became only the second cartoon character to be given a star on the Hollywood Walk of Fame. Mickey Mouse was the first.

Sources
Adapted from: http://www.neatorama.com/2010/11/08/a-brief-history-of-bugs-bunny/
http://en.wikipedia.org/wiki/Bugs_Bunny#mediaviewer/File:Classic_bugsbunny.png
http://www.infoplease.com/biography/var/bugsbunny.html

Understanding Biographies

1. Who drew the first pictures of Bugs Bunny in his present form?
    - A   Tex Avery
    - B   Ben Hardaway
    - C   Mel Blanc
    - D   Charlie Thorson

2. According to the text which statement is CORRECT?
    - A   Bugs Bunny was awarded an Oscar on his first nomination.
    - B   Bugs Bunny had a top-rating TV shows for almost 30 years.
    - C   Bugs Bunny received his star on the Walk of Fame before Mickey Mouse.
    - D   Bugs Bunny was voted in as America's top screen character in 1967.

3. What was added to Bugs Bunny's character in 1940?
    - A   buck teeth
    - B   a carrot
    - C   a voice
    - D   a gun

4. Which words from the text is an example of a simile?
    - A   it was like an explosion (1937)
    - B   the rabbit was just Daffy Duck in a rabbit suit (1938)
    - C   a grey and white rabbit with large buckteeth (1939)
    - D   he was a sly looking rascal (1940)

5. The emerging Bugs Bunny character could best be described as
    - A   gallant and theatrical
    - B   cheeky and flamboyant
    - C   rude and indifferent
    - D   brave and blunt

6. The text states: *Bugs's debut as a star was the 1940 short **A Wild Hare**.*
    What is meant by the word debut in this context?
    - A   the moment a rabbit character superseded a duck character
    - B   the early drawings of a rabbit as a cartoon character
    - C   the first performance of Bugs Bunny's in a major role
    - D   the beginning of Bugs Bunny as a debonair cartoon character

7. When Mel Blanc saw the Bugs Bunny as depicted in *A Wild Hare* he was
    - A   uneasy
    - B   sceptical
    - C   perplexed
    - D   enthused

8. The words of Bugs Bunny, "What's up Doc?" could best be described as a
    - A   catchphrase
    - B   cliché
    - C   motto
    - D   slogan

Lit Tip 19 – Improve your Literacy skills   **The suffix,ism**

The suffix *ism* is quite common. As abstract nouns *ism* words can refer to:
1. an action or the result of an action (baptism, criticism, tourism)
2. a characteristic (optimism, heroism)
3. a belief or ideal (communism, Hinduism, capitalism)
4. a discrimination (racism, ageism,feminism)
5. a condition (alcoholism, autism)
Which noun would you use to describe: the religion of Buddha? _____
                                       something that is true? _____
                                       being treated as a favourite _____

The Photograph

Roy had been doing an inspection of their new furnished flat. He had found the photograph in the bottom drawer of a bedside cupboard in what was to be his room.

It all started when he distractedly opened and closed the three empty drawers several times in turn. It was when he was opening and closing the bottom drawer for the second time he thought he heard a slight rustling sound from inside. When he opened he heard nothing but when he closed the drawer he heard the same rustling sound. It rubbed on something on its way in. He opened the drawer again. He frowned and squatted down, looked inside and felt around but found nothing.

Slowly he pushed it shut, and the same noise came again. He knelt down on the floor, pulled the drawer right out and saw something stuck near a runner. He reached in and slowly drew it from where it had become lodged.

It was a small, bent black and white photo, showing a grave in a cemetery in wintertime. It looked familiar. There was a headstone on the grave. Most of the inscription was unclear. A female's name was inscribed there - Andrea. No family name.

Roy couldn't see the date clearly so he moved over to the window. Outside the drizzle was turning the light into a dreary grey. By tilting the photo towards the insipid, fading light and squinting he could he could just make out the dates: 1997 - 2007.

1997, he thought - the year he was born.

He could vaguely see the lines of letters of an epitaph. He wiped the dust off the print with his fingers but the lettering was still not clear.

The girl had been ten years old when she died. Was he about to occupy the room of a dead person? A cold shiver ran down his spine.

Roy looked out the window. Light was ebbing from the autumn day. For reasons he could not explain he felt heavy-hearted.

Understanding Narratives

1. What is the most likely reason Roy was in the room with the bedside table?
   - A he was looking for a photo
   - B he was investigating his new room
   - C he had come in out of the rain
   - D he was an intruder

2. What did Roy have to do to retrieve the photo?
   - A feel to the back of the lowest drawer
   - B take all three drawers from the cupboard
   - C fully remove the lowest drawer
   - D slide the bottom drawer in and out several times

3. When a *cold shiver* (paragraph 8) ran down Roy's spine it suggests he was
   - A catching a chill
   - B feeling the autumn cold in the air
   - C getting excited about his find
   - D stressed by something he couldn't explain

4. Which word best describes the tone of the text? (Check **Lit Tip 8**.)
   - A dramatic
   - B cheery
   - C sombre
   - D peaceful

5. The mood (or atmosphere) the text creates is one of (Check **Lit Tip 20**.)
   - A gloom
   - B peace
   - C excitement
   - D fear

6. Roy is described as feeling *heavy-hearted* (last paragraph)?
   This suggests Roy
   - A has feelings of distrust
   - B is involved in deep thought
   - C is obsessed with one idea
   - D has a vague awareness of sadness

7. What alerted Roy to the presence of something in the cupboard?
   - A the drawers were difficult to open or shut
   - B he heard a sound when closing the lowest drawer
   - C the drawers were heavy to pull out
   - D one drawer wouldn't shut completely

8. A suitable alternate title for the passage would be
   - A The discovery
   - B Roy fixes a cupboard
   - C Autumn days
   - D Andrea

Lit Tip 20 – Improve your Literacy skills   **Mood (or atmosphere)**

Did you have a problem with Q 5? In fiction mood refers to the feelings the text creates in the reader's mind. Writers use the setting, descriptions and words to create a certain mood or atmosphere. In a story or novel mood can change.

Mood can be expressed in such terms as dark, light, rushed, suspenseful and chaotic.

Read the **Practice page** passage again. (*The Cave Dwellers*)

Circle the word that best describes the mood in this passage.

mysterious   oppressive   hopeful   relaxed   threatening

In plays or films mood can be created with the help of dialogue, sets, lights and music.

Beyond the Black Stump

Anyone who has spent anytime in the outback will tell you there are plenty of good reasons to live elsewhere. Firstly, there is the distance from civilization, which according to most people living in towns along the Darling River will, at least, mean Dubbo but more likely the state capital - Sydney - 400 km away. These once thriving paddle–steamer towns such as Bourke, Brewarrina and Wilcannia have been passed by as the younger population drifted away, which is a cause for regret.

There are the winters which are cold, even chilly, as the icy winds from the Red Centre blast sand and dust upon one and all without discrimination. The locals call them lazy winds - they don't go around the inhabitants but they pass straight through. In a bad year winter can extend well into spring.

Spring is the lead up to summer with heatwaves and fires against a backdrop of prolonged drought. The last drought lasted ten years. The river becomes so low that the once busy paddle steamers would not have managed to come more than a few kilometres up-stream from the junction with the Murray River. There are more logs and snags in the river than there are sandbars - or often water.

Then there are the flies that come in droves as soon as there is a few mills of rain that accidentally pour out of a pathetic summer storm. The flies, little black bush flies, seem to burst from the bush as if on command. They are about half a centimetre long and can seem to land unexpected on any part of the human body that has any semblance of moisture. They make great pulsating clouds on the  backs of anyone who ventures from the security of a well-screened house.

These little black devils go for the eyes, the nose and any mouth that stays open for more than a nanosecond. These creatures can be the ultimate distraction. Don't drive with the windows down! Caught in a swarm a person can very quickly become demented.

Try escaping them by going for a swim in the local weir. Doesn't work. You can swim underwater for as long as your air lasts, but the second you break the surface they use your head as a landing platform. Splashing and thrashing about just makes you less resistant to their onslaught.

Source unknown

Understanding Reports

Circle a letter to answer questions 1 to 8.

1. The text is most likely intended to

   A   entertain   B   enlighten   C   forewarn   D   inform

2. The writer makes this comment regarding the drift of the younger population from Darling River towns as *a cause for regret*.
   The term a cause for regret is an example of

   A   a fact   B   a euphemism   C   a slang term   D   an opinion

3. The writer feels the most annoying thing about living beyond the black stump is

   A   the isolation of western towns   B   the unavoidable swarms of flies

   C   the extremes of weather   D   the degradation of the Darling River

4. Which method does the writer suggest may be one to escape the flies?

   A   take a trip to Dubbo   B   go for a swim in the local weir

   C   stay inside a screened house   D   keep out of summer storms

5. What reason does the writer give for describing the winter winds as lazy?

   A   they have little strength

   B   they are easily halted by any obstacle

   C   they only survive for a short season each year

   D   they pass straight through inhabitants instead of going around them

6. What is the writer suggesting when he implores people not to drive with the windows down?

   A   flies in the car may be the cause of erratic and dangerous driving

   B   flies will become disoriented inside a moving car

   C   flies could be unintentionally transported to other western towns

   D   flies removed from river towns need moisture to survive

7. By using the word *nanosecond* (paragraph 5) the writer is purposely using

   A   a fact   B   a euphemism   C   an exaggeration   D   a metaphor

8. According to the text what is a major problem for outback towns in summer?

   A   storms that bring little rain   B   the sudden influx of little black flies

   C   no paddle-steamer services   D   icy winds carrying red dust

---

Lit Tip 21 – Improve your Literacy skills   **The @ (at) symbol**

The @ symbol was a rarely used key on a typewriter but has become a very common symbol in modern electronic communication thanks to email addresses and Twitter handles. It is called a *snail* by the Italians and a *monkey* by the Dutch.

It was originally used in accounting as a short-cut way to write *each at* : 4 apples @ 7c.

It is believed it may have had its origins as a small *a* inside a larger *e*.

It was not included on the keyboard of early typewriters but was included in a 1889 model and became common in the 1900 onwards. It is now universally included on computer keyboards.

Write an address you use containing the @ symbol. _____

Understanding Year 7 Comprehension
A. Horsfield © Five Senses Education © W. Marlin

Read the poem *Andy's Gone With Cattle.*

Andy's Gone With Cattle

Our Andy's gone to battle now
'Gainst Drought, the red marauder,
Our Andy's gone with cattle now
Across the Queensland border.

He's left us in dejection now;
Our hearts with him are roving.
It's dull on this selection now,
Since Andy went a-droving.

Who now shall wear the cheerful face
In times when things are slackest?
And who shall whistle round the place
When Fortune frowns her blackest?

Oh, who shall cheek the squatter now
When he comes round us snarling?
His tongue is growing hotter now
Since Andy cross'd the Darling*.

The gates are out of order now,
In storms the `riders'** rattle,
For far across the border now
Our Andy's gone with cattle.

Poor Aunty's looking thin and white;
And Uncle's cross with worry;
And poor old Blucher howls all night
Since Andy left Macquarie*.

Oh, may the showers in torrents fall,
And all the tanks run over:
And may the grass grow green and tall
In pathways of the drover.

And may good angels send the rain
On desert stretches sandy;
And when the summer comes again
God grant 'twill bring us Andy.

Droving near Walgett NSW

** gate supports

* rivers in western NSW

Henry Lawson (1867-1922)

Photo source: http://en.wikipedia.org/wiki/Stock_route

Understanding Poetry

Circle a letter or write an answer for questions 1 to 8.

1. Who is the most likely narrator of the poem?
   - A Henry Lawson
   - B a squatter
   - C one of Andy's family
   - D old Blucher

2. What two feelings are the people on the selection feeling while Andy's out droving?
   - A loneliness and vulnerability
   - B satisfaction and enthusiasm
   - C freedom and anticipation
   - D despair and gloom

3. Other than the return of Andy what do the people on the selection want most?
   - A the gates fixed
   - B good soaking rains
   - C someone to confront the squatter
   - D Uncle to stop worrying

4. When the poet speaks of *the red marauder* (stanza 1) he is most likely referring to
   - A cattle rustlers
   - B desert sands
   - C wild animals
   - D dry summer weather

5. Andy is most likely droving the cattle in
   - A a northerly direction
   - B a westerly direction
   - C an easterly direction
   - D a southerly direction

6. Which of these lines from the poem is an example of a metaphor?
   - A Poor Aunty's looking thin and white
   - B It's dull on this selection now
   - C His tongue is growing hotter now
   - D And who shall whistle round the place

7. Which word best describes Andy when he's back home on the selection?
   - A moody
   - B involved
   - C irritable
   - D cheerful

8. The line, *When Fortune frowns her blackest*, (stanza 3) is an example of
   - A a euphemism
   - B country jargon
   - C personification
   - D hyperbole

Lit Tip 22 – Improve your Literacy skills　　　　**Know your genre types**

Genre refers to a type of literature (or art or music).
Literature is often divided into a number of different types (or kinds).
Some common fiction genres
humour - texts that are intended to amuse the reader
fantasy - texts that use magic and witchcraft in their plots
science fiction - stories based on developments in science and based in the future
crime/detective - stories about the solving of a crime
western - a story set in remote country with cowboys as characters
horror - fiction which evokes feelings of dread or fear
Not all fiction fits neatly into a particular genre. Stories can overlap genres.
What is your favourite genre? _____

Understanding Year 7 Comprehension
A. Horsfield © Five Senses Education © W. Marlin

What are Electric Ants?

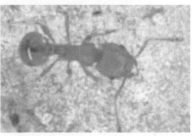

1 Close up of an electric ant.

Electric ants are part of a group called tramp ants. Tramp ants are a diverse group of invasive ant species which have become established widely across the globe. They can arrive in Australia through many transport methods. Once here they can affect the environment, social and cultural values, and human health.

Tramp ants get their name from their ability to spread via cargo transported by humans. At least six tramp ant species have national priority for management because of their potential impact on biodiversity. Two tramp ant species have quite hurtful stings: the fire ant and electric ant.

Electric ants arrived from South America via various routes. They have a painful sting. They are very small, about 1.5 mm long (much smaller than the common black ant), and brown in colour. They are slow moving.

Electric ants have a serious impact upon Australia economy and environment. They also have an effect on the lifestyle of people who live in areas infected with electric ants.

The Economy

Electric ants 'farm' plant pests such as scale, mealybugs and aphids in exchange for their sugars. These pests can cause plant dieback. Farmworkers and farm animals can be affected by the stings of electric ants.

Environment

Electric ants cause declines in native insect population and small 'animals'. Where they exist in large numbers very few other creatures exist.

Lifestyle

When electric ants sting they inject a venom causing a painful, itchy rash and possibly an allergic reaction. They are not aggressive but can be defensive if disturbed. They can put a stop to some outdoor activities such as games and barbecues.

Queensland Government

Biosecurity Queensland

Electric ant restricted area

This area is a designated electric ant restricted area and strict movement controls apply.

For more information call 13 25 23.

3 Electric ant warning sign North Qld
Photo: A Horsfield

2 Electric ant on a human arm hair

Electric ants don't nest but use spaces under rocks, in pot plants, in trees, in leaf litter and in rotten tree limbs. They can invade homes. Electric ants are regarded as one of the world's 100 worst invasive species and are a serious environmental and urban pest.

Sources: http://www.environment.gov.au/biodiversity/invasive-species/insects-and-other-invertebrates/trampants, http://en.wikipedia.org/wiki/Electric_antElectric ants information sheet: National Electric Ant Eradication Program

Understanding Explanations

Circle a letter to answer questions 1 to 8.

1. The bite of an electric ant is **unlikely** to cause
   - A itchiness
   - B a rash
   - C death
   - D an allergic reaction

2. According to the text, electric ants can drastically affect lifestyle by preventing Australians from
   - A gardening
   - B farming
   - C socialising
   - D travelling

3. Tramp ant species have a *national priority for management* because they
   - A have a sting that can be hurtful
   - B can effect Australia's biodiversity
   - C can invade home gardens
   - D manage other pests as a food source

4. According to the text which statement about electric ants is CORRECT?
   - A Electric ants are indigenous to Australia.
   - B Electric ants came to Australia directly from South America.
   - C Electric ants spread from Australia to other countries.
   - D Electric ants arrived in Australia after passing through other countries.

5. When describing the government's reaction to electric ant infestations an appropriate description would be:
   - A lacking enthusiasm
   - B initiating a rational response
   - C a misdirected effort
   - D responding with unnecessary vigour

6. The main benefit of **photo 2** (lower left hand corner) of the text is to show the
   - A relative size of the ant
   - B fearlessness of the ant
   - C suffering the ant can cause
   - D aggressiveness of the ant

7. How many tramp ant species are believed to be in Australia?
   - A only one
   - B just two
   - C no more than four
   - D at least six

8. The word *animals* (paragraph 6) is in inverted commas. This is to indicate that the word is
   - A intended to be inclusive of a range of creatures
   - B incorrect in this context
   - C restricted in meaning to mammals
   - D not relevant to insects

Lit Tip 23 – Improve your Literacy skills   **Shades of meaning**

It is important in writing to have the word that best reflects your intended meaning.
These words indicate freedom from agitation: calm, serene, tranquil, placid, peaceful.
calm: describes someone or a situation that is free from worry.
serene: describes someone that has an 'inner' peace
tranquil: often describes places that are free from noise or disturbance
placid: describes someone who is not easily upset or worried
peaceful: often describes an absence of disturbance or conflict
Choose the best word for the spaces.
Her eyes were closed and she looked _____.
After the storm the seas were _____. (Answers may vary.)

Understanding Year 7 Comprehension
A. Horsfield © Five Senses Education © W. Marlin

The Reconnoitre

Mr Case led them through the thorny bushes in a crouch sprint to the fence, whose posts seemed to lean precariously at a variety of angles. He held apart the rusty wires so that Nikki and Sandy could clamber through and across to a sidewall of the building.

Meanwhile the mist coming up the valley was getting thicker carrying with it the scent of eucalyptus from the gums along the creek. They were now no more than shadowy shapes. The grass beneath their feet was damp and cool.

Mr Case shuffled past and beckoned them to follow him around the end of the wall of the dark house. Here was a jumble of old sheds and lean-tos piled up with rubbish and abandoned farm equipment of another era. A rusty plough, a wheelbarrow with no bottom and lengths of old chain looped through the short winter grass. For such a large, once-imposing house on a block of prime river land up this close, it looked as if it was surround by a rubbish tip.

Leading them cautiously past rotting, damp smelling bales of hay and past a small heap of discarded tractor tyres Mr Case made his way along the back wall of the building.

They came to a low, broken granite wall that had been part of a washhouse for the original owners. The three of them were able to creep up to it with the benefit of decreasing light without being seen.

The mist turned into a light drizzle. Nikki ran her hand over her black hair to rid it of the accumulating moisture. It was then they heard a dog growl. Then a light came on in a small window.

Understanding Narratives

Circle a letter or write an answer for questions 1 to 8.

1. What is the meaning of reconnoitre?
   - A   to make a military-style observation of a place
   - B   to reconcile an action with the reason for that action
   - C   to look for evidence of a house occupation
   - D   to undertake an illegal activity

2. The most likely explanation of the trio's behaviour?
   - A   they were participating in a surprise visit
   - B   they were returning home late
   - C   they were trespassing
   - D   they were trying to get out of the rain

3. Mr Case, Nikki and Sandy were aware that the house was
   - A   temporarily vacant
   - B   permanently abandoned
   - C   most likely guarded
   - D   possibly occupied

4. What was the first smell the trio encountered? (Check out **Lit Tip 25**.)
   - A   the scent of eucalyptus trees
   - B   the damp bales of hay
   - C   the rubbish behind the house
   - D   the smell of the river

5. Which word best reflects the mood (atmosphere) of the passage? (Check out **Lit Tip 20**.)
   - A   despair
   - B   suspenseful
   - C   fearful
   - D   chaotic

6. In which order did the trio encounter the following features?
   1. the out-houses
   2. a barbed wire fence
   3. a low granite wall
   4. discarded tractor tyres
   - A   **2, 4, 1, 3**
   - B   **3, 4, 2, 1**
   - C   **2, 1, 4, 3**
   - D   **1, 2, 3, 4**

7. The fact the house, surrounded by rubbish, sat on a prime piece of real estate could best be considered (Check out **Lit Tip 20**.)
   - A   prophetic
   - B   significant
   - C   symbolic
   - D   ironic

8. Which word in the text means *walked without lifting the feet fully from the ground*?
   Write your answer on the line. _____

Lit Tip 24 – Improve your Literacy skills   **Italics**

Italics is a style of typeface in which letters are slanted to the right.
1. Italics are most commonly used for the names of publications (books, magazines).
We always buy the *Sydney Morning Herald*.
2. Italics may be used for the names of ships and aircraft.
There is no danger that the *Titanic* will sink!
3. They are used for foreign words in English text. It is not good-bye but *au revoir*.
4. They can be used to emphasise a word. *You* think I'm a moron!
Underline the words that should be italicised.
1. The Spanish word for cat is gato.   **2.** I have never seen the movie Star Wars.

Understanding Year 7 Comprehension
A. Horsfield © Five Senses Education © W. Marlin

Read the report *Ho Chi Minh Mausoleum.*

Ho Chi Minh Mausoleum

The Ho Chi Minh Mausoleum is a large memorial in Hanoi, Vietnam. It is located in the centre of Ba Dinh Square which is the place where Vietnamese leader Ho Chi Minh read his Declaration of Independence in 1945.

Visitors line up to enter the mausoleum. Photo: A Horsfield

Ho Chi Min (1890 - 1969) was the Vietnamese leader of his nation's independence. A nationalist and revolutionary, he founded the Vietnamese Communist Party and was its leader during the first 50 years of its existence. He guided the Vietnamese people against Japan in the Second World War and in its struggles for Vietnamese independence and unification, including conflicts with France and the United States, which the Vietnamese call the American War.

Minh served as president of the Democratic Republic of Vietnam from 1945 until his death. He is memorialised by the Hanoi mausoleum and the renaming of Vietnam's principal city from Saigon to Ho Chi Minh City.

Minh's wish was to be cremated, and to have his ashes buried on the hills of the North, the Centre, and the South of Vietnam. Yet, in honour of his huge dedication for the country and for the love of all Vietnamese for him, the successive Communist Governments decided to keep his body so that he can see the whole country's reunion, and future generations can visit him.

Accordingly, on 2 September, 1973, work commenced on his mausoleum in Ba Dinh Square, and was completed in 1975.

The embalmed body of Ho Chi Minh is preserved in the cooled, central hall of the mausoleum, which is protected by a military honour guard. The body lies in a glass case with dim lights. The mausoleum is closed occasionally while work is done to restore and preserve the body but it is normally open daily from 09:00 to 12:00 to the public. Lines of visitors, including visiting foreign dignitaries, pay their respects daily.

Rules regarding dress and behaviour are enforced by staff and guards. Legs must be covered (no shorts or miniskirts). Visitors must be silent, and walk in two lines. Hands must not be in pockets, nor arms crossed. Smoking, drinking, eating, photography and video taping are also not permitted inside the mausoleum. Ho Chi Minh is known by the Vietnamese as 'Uncle Ho'.

Sources: From ionformation available at the site, http://en.wikipedia.org/wiki/Ho_Chi_Minh_Mausoleum

Understanding Reports

Circle a letter to answer questions 1 to 8.

1. A mausoleum is the name given to
- A   a place housing a holy or sacred person
- B   a stately building housing a tomb
- C   a burial room attached to a church
- D   an underground cemetery containing many tombs

2. Ho Chi Minh is memorialised in Vietnam by his mausoleum and by
- A   being leader of the Communist Party
- B   having his ashes spread across the country
- C   winning the war against South Vietnam
- D   the renaming of Saigon in South Vietnam

3. Which word best describes the feeling visitors most likely feel in the mausoleum?
- A   threatened   B   excited   C   sombre   D   cheerful

4. The government ignored Minh's wish to be cremated because
- A   the ashes had to be buried in three remote, separate places
- B   citizens wanted an opportunity to show their gratitude for Minh's achievements
- C   they wanted foreign dignitaries to visit their great leader
- D   a mausoleum had been built where his body was to lie in state

5. The last line states: *Ho Chi Minh is known by the Vietnamese as 'Uncle Ho'.*
Uncle Ho is most likely used by the Vietnamese as term of
- A   respect   B   ridicule   C   scorn   D   awe

6. Visitors viewing the body of Ho Chi Minh in the mausoleum
- A   should talk very softly   B   should cross their arms while inside
- C   must walk through in two lines   D   may take photographs once inside

7. In which year did Ho Chi Minh cease to be president of Vietnam?
- A   1945   B   1969   C   1973   D   1975

8. Look at the photograph. Which word adequately describes the building?
- A   artistic   B   regal
- C   delicate   D   imposing

Lit Tip 25 – Improve your Literacy skills   **Improving narratives 1**

Often in narratives writers focus on what can be seen.
We have 4 other senses. They are: _____. _____. _____, _____
It is important in narratives (and descriptions) to include text that focuses on other senses. What sense does this passage focus on?
Fiona made her way across the bare damp boards of the chilly room. Parts of the floor were so smooth that once or twice she nearly slipped. Finally she reached the window. With her finger she rubbed a lop-sided circle in the frost and grime that covered the entire surface. Then before putting her finger in her warm mouth she rubbed it clean on the coarse fabric of her coat.*
Write your answer on the line. _____

(* adapted from Creative Writing Years 5 /6 A. Horsfield Excel 2004)

Understanding Year 7 Comprehension
A. Horsfield © Five Senses Education © W. Marlin

Bring Back the Rubbish

Mt Everest climbers will each be made to bring back at least 8 kg of rubbish on their way down, under new rules to remove a growing garbage problem on the world's highest peak.

Nepalese officials said the new rules were part of a package of measures.

A spokesman for Nepal's tourism ministry, said climbers who failed to return litter to a special government office to be established at base camp would be punished. "The government has decided in order to clean up Mount Everest, each member of an expedition must bring back at least eight kilos of garbage, apart from their own trash," he said.

"Our earlier efforts have not been very effective. This time if they don't bring back garbage we will take legal action and penalise them."

The growing number of climbers attempting to scale the 8 848m peak, first climbed by Sir Edmund Hillary and Tenzing Norgay (1953), has led to increased pollution, with an estimated 50 tonnes of rubbish left on the slopes each year, environmental groups say.

The garbage, which can date back several decades, includes oxygen and cooking gas canisters, old tents, food packaging, human waste, a helicopter and several corpses, which do not fully decompose in the extreme cold. 2013 was the busiest in Everest's history, with 810 climbers attempting to scale the Himalayan peak from Nepal. More attempted the climb from the Tibetan side.

The overcrowding came into sharp focus when a brawl erupted at about 7 300m between European climbers and Nepalese Sherpas. A Swiss climber, was forced to flee from the mountain after Sherpas threw rocks at his tent. Other western climbers intervened to save him.

Tourist ministry officials said soldiers and police will now be stationed at base camp to resolve any security issues.

Adding to overcrowding fears, last month Nepal — which earns millions of dollars a year from climbers — said it would slash the cost of permits from about $25 000 per climber, down to $12 000 to attract many more climbers and increase revenue for the government.

Adapted from The Times 4/03/14
http://news.discovery.com/earth/nepaul-to-force-everest-climbers-to-collect-rubbish-140303.htm
http://www.theguardian.com/world/2014/feb/14/nepal-slashes-cost-climbing-mount-everest

Understanding Reports

Circle a letter or write an answer for questions 1 to 8.

1. How much rubbish are returning climbers expected to carry back?
   A at least 8 kilograms
   B as much as they can carry
   C 8 kilograms per climbing team
   D their own trash plus 8 kilograms of other litter

2. According to the text what is the heaviest thing that has been 'left' on Mt Everest?
   Write your answer on the line. _____

3. To ensure there are no disputes on the mountain the Nepalese authorities will
   A increase the fine levels for disturbances
   B take legal action against those who get involved in disputes
   C station police and soldiers at the base camp
   D raise the fee for climbing the mountain to stop overcrowding

4. The lowering of permit fees to climb Mt Everest is likely to result in
   A an increased number of disputes between Sherpas and climbers
   B the removal of greater amounts of rubbish
   C readily available support for inexperienced climbers
   D less back-up services at the base camp

5. The most likely reason human waste (faeces) is part of the problem is because
   A there are no toilets on the mountains
   B human waste is polluting the waterways and soil
   C climbers don't take care to be environmentally sound
   D human waste doesn't decompose in the freezing temperatures

6. The most likely reason many climbers climb Mt Everest is because
   A of the fellowship of other climbers   B it is the world's highest peak
   C they can assist in the clean-up   D it is an adventure of few risks

7. What would be a suitable synonym for *climb* as used in the article?
   A scale   B clamber   C conquer   D mount

8. The second paragraph is an example of
   A direct speech   B indirect speech

Lit Tip 26 – Improve your Literacy skills   **Improving narratives 2**

Often in narratives writers focus on what can be seen. (Check out **Lit Tip 25**)
It is important in narratives (and descriptions) to include text that focuses on other senses. What sense does this text focus on?
When the laughter of the other campers finally ceased Ken expected silence. But instead of silence the bush outside was full of strange sounds.
A bird's mournful cry could be heard in a nearby whispering tree. The monotonous trickle of the creek was like the incessant arguing of a distant group of children. Then he isolated the buzzing and hissing of strange insects, the rustling in the dry grass by the tent where he was to sleep. He even became aware of his own breathing.*
Write your answer on the line. _____

(* adapted from Creative Writing Years 5 /6 A. Horsfield Excel 2004)

Understanding Year 7 Comprehension
A. Horsfield © Five Senses Education © W. Marlin

Idiom

Idiom is group of words established by usage as having a meaning not deducible from those of the individual words, for example, hit the sack.

Because idioms can mean something different from what the words mean it is difficult for someone not very good at speaking English to use them properly. Idioms then are words, phrases, or expressions that cannot be taken literally. In other words, when used in everyday language, they have a meaning other than the basic one you would find in the dictionary.

An expression that doesn't exactly mean what the words say.

Example:

She spilled the beans.
(she talked too much and told the secret)

Every language has its own idioms. Learning them makes understanding and using a language a lot easier and more fun!

For example, "break a leg" is a common idiom. Its literal meaning is something like go and break a bone in your leg. Its idiomatic meaning has something to do with doing your best and do it well. Often, actors tell each other to "break a leg" before they perform on the stage.

It is common to say: It's raining cats and dogs. Literally: cats and dogs are falling from the sky. Idiomatically (or figuratively): it is raining heavily.

An idiom is generally a colloquial metaphor — a term requiring some basic knowledge, information, or experience, to use only within a culture, where people possess a common cultural background. Therefore, idioms are not considered part of the language, but part of the culture. As culture typically is localised, idioms often are useless beyond their local context. Nevertheless, some idioms can be more universal than others, and the meaning can be _____(5)_____out.

Idioms can often be very difficult to understand. You may be able to guess the meaning from context but if not, it is not easy to know the meaning. Many idioms, for instance, come from favourite traditional British activities such as fighting, sailing, hunting and playing games. As well as being quite specialist in meaning, some of the words in idioms were used two or three hundred years ago and can be a little obscure.

How to Learn Idioms

It is best to learn idioms as you do vocabulary. In other words, select and actively learn idioms which will be useful to you.

Sources: http://www.idiomsite.com/ http://www.watchungschools.com/
http://www.heathermeloche.com/What%20is%20an%20Idiom.htm
http://www.grammar-monster.com/glossary/idiom.htm

Understanding Explanations

Circle a letter or write an answer for questions 1 to 8.

1. The problem with idiom for students learning English is that
   - A   to understand the idiom the student needs to know two languages
   - B   it takes longer to master the language than the idiom
   - C   the context in which the idiom exists is purposely left ambiguous
   - D   the words have a meaning other than the literal meaning

2. Which group of people would have the most difficulty in understanding idiom?
   - A   people born a long time ago
   - B   people who are involved in British sports
   - C   people who use English as a second language
   - D   people who perform on stages

3. Sally *lets the cat out the bag.*
   This idiomatic expression really means Sally:
   - A   gave away a secret
   - B   is kind to cats
   - C   finds things to do
   - D   has bought a cat

4. Which of these idiomatic expressions means *a lot of money*?
   - A   at sixes and sevens
   - B   an arm and a leg
   - C   in seventh heaven
   - D   firing on all cylinders

5. A word has been deleted from the text.
   Which word would be best suited to the space (5)?

   Write your answer on the line. _____

6. Language that is *colloquial* is language that is used
   - A   for precise instruction
   - B   when addressing an audience
   - C   in everyday speech
   - D   when reporting an emergency

7. The expression ***I'll eat my hat*** is intended to show
   - A   surprise
   - B   hunger
   - C   stupidity
   - D   rudeness

8. Idiomatic expressions would be inappropriate in a
   - A   stage play
   - B   job application
   - C   graphic novel
   - D   children's story

Lit Tip 27 – Improve your Literacy skills   **When to use an ellipsis**

An ellipsis (plural: ellipses) is a set of dots (. . .) that indicate that something is left out or not said. Ellipses have three dots, **no more!**
They can be used to
- show a pause: "You're certain . . . " said Paul quietly.
- show hesitation: I meant . . . I mean . . . what I really meant . . .
- indicate words omitted on purpose but the intended meaning is clear.
  Dad said, "You didn't finish the mowing, so . . . " (Dad is making a bit of a threat.)

Note: Commas or full stops do **not** follow an ellipsis.
Where could be an appropriate place for an ellipsis in this sentence? (Use an oblique line.)
Habib thought and thought and then thought some more.
Ellipses are often overused in some students' writing. Use them sparingly.
Check out **Lit Tip 10** for the correct use of dashes. Dashes show interrupted speech.

Understanding Year 7 Comprehension
A. Horsfield © Five Senses Education © W. Marlin

How to Write a Descriptive Passage

A descriptive passage is a passage that provides location and mood (atmosphere). Mood is used to create feelings or emotional responses in readers through words by describing things such as places, people and events (See Lit Tip 20). Decide if the description is going to be from a first person (the writer uses the pronoun, I) or a third person point of view.

Descriptive passages are often used in fiction and non-fiction writing, to help readers into the world of the author. They rarely stand-alone. Though there are no hard and fast rules for how exactly these passages should be structured, there are several suggestions that can make an effective and appealing descriptive passage or even a paragraph.

Descriptive passages include details that appeal to the five senses: sight, taste, touch, smell, and hearing, in order to give the best possible description to the reader. The reader should feel as if they can experience and 'feel' (emotionally) what is being described.

Descriptive passages should include some figurative language. It is important to include similes and metaphors when writing a descriptive passage. These literary devices give impact to the passages if used properly (and not overused). Other options are personification, hyperbole, repetition, alliteration and onomatopoeia. Take care to avoid clichés. Include descriptive adjectives to modify nouns and adverbs to modify verbs.

Resist using overworked words such as nice, good, awful, pretty, terrible or awesome. Words like these carry very little meaning or impact and do not improve the reader's mental picture. They do very little for the writing.

A concluding sentence may not be necessary for a descriptive passage as it is usually part of a longer piece of writing. However the reader should be able to make a mental picture of the subject described, and draw an accurate picture of it in his or her mind. Keep descriptions sounding vital and if possible, original.

Adapted from: http://www.wikihow.com/Write-a-Descriptive-Paragraph
http://web.clark.edu/martpe/descriptive%20paragr.htm

Understanding Procedures

Circle a letter or write an answer for questions 1 to 8.

1.

> Randy sniffed twice. The fumes from the bus were acrid but there was something else.
> It wasn't a foul odour. It was a whiff of sharp scent that stung the insides of his nostrils.

What sense has the writer focussed on in the above descriptive text?
Write your answer on the line. _____

2. A descriptive passage may not need a concluding sentence because the passage

    A   doesn't involve any action
    B   contains sufficient informational text
    C   loses focus with the added text
    D   is usually part of a longer text

3. The word emotionally is in brackets (emotionally) in paragraph 3. (Check out Lit Tip 18)
This is because the

    A   writer wanted to draw attention to the word
    B   word is a synonym which needs an explanation
    C   word feel has a second meaning relating to touch
    D   use of emotive words is important in descriptions

4. According to the text which adjective would be the least appropriate for a description of a party?

    A   tedious   B   good   C   crowded   D   noisy

5. What literary device does the writer suggest other writers should avoid?

    A   repetition   B   metaphors   C   hyperbole   D   clichés

6. Which sentence is the topic sentence in paragraph 4?

    A   Descriptive passages should include some figurative language.
    B   It is important to include similes and metaphors when writing a descriptive passage.
    C   These literary devices give impact to the passages if used properly.
    D   Take care to avoid clichés.

7. A suitable synonym for the word *location* as used in the text (paragraph 1) would be

    A   movement   B   setting   C   position   D   space

8. Descriptive passages may be described as rarely being stand-alone passages.
This suggest that such passages

    A   have little place in literature
    B   do not make a lot of sense
    C   work best supporting other text
    D   need to be at the start of a narrative

Lit Tip 28 – Improve your Literacy skills   **What is a metonym?**

A metonym is a word (or phrase) that is used to stand for another word or object.
We often refer to cars as *wheels*, the police as the *boys in blue*, the Australian Government as *Canberra* and hired help as *hands*.
Metonyms are a literary device that can make your writing more interesting as well as breaking up any awkwardness in having to repeat the same word too many times.
Complete these with a suitable metonym.
1. I want you to listen to me so give me your _____. (4 letters)
2. The monarchy is good for the kingdom so we remain loyal to the c _ _ _ _ .
You don't have to remember the word metonym to use them in your writing.

Understanding Year 7 Comprehension
A. Horsfield © Five Senses Education © W. Marlin

Night Mystery

My father, Joe Clear, used to tell me stories. In 1888 he had been a sailor at the age of seventeen.

He used to tell me a curious story about Southampton. As a child I received it as gospel truth. It may have been true for all that.

One season coming into port he could find no bed in his favourite boarding house and was obliged to go further along the windy waste of terraces and signs and found a lonely house with a VACANT sign stuck out to fish in customers. In he went and was met by a grey-faced woman in her middle years, who gave him a bed in the basement of the house.

In the middle of the night he awoke, thinking he had heard someone breathing in the room. Startled, and with that extreme wakefulness that attends to such panic, he heard a groan, and someone lay in the bed beside in the dark.

He lit his candle from a tinderbox. There was no one to be seen. But he saw the bedclothes and the mattress depressed where a heavy person lay. He leaped up from the bed and called out but there was no reply. It was then he noticed a terrible sense of hunger such as not had afflicted an Irishman since the dark famine. He rushed to the door but to his amazement it was locked against him.

Now he was greatly outraged. 'Let me out, let me out!' he called, both terrified and affronted.

How dare the old hag lock him in! He banged and banged and finally the landlady came and unlocked it. She apologised and said it must have been unwittingly locked against thieves. He told her about the disturbance but she only smiled and said nothing, and then went up to her own quarters. He thought he had caught from her a strange smell of leaves, of underfloor and undergrowth, like she had been crawling through the woodland. Then there was calm, and he snuffed out the candle and tried to sleep.

The same thing happened a little while later. He leapt up again and lit his candle and went to the door. It was locked again! Again he had a deep gnawing of hunger in his belly. For some reason, maybe because of her extreme strangeness he couldn't bear to call the landlady, and sweating, he spent the night in a chair.

When morning broke and he awoke, and dressed, and went to the door it was open.

Adapted from: https://www.allenandunwin.com/_uploads/BookPdf/Extract/9780571239610.pdf
From: The Secret Scripture 2 Sebastian Barry faber and faber 2009 ed pp 6 – 7
My thanks for permission received to reproduce this text.

Understanding Narratives

1. Which part of Joe Clear's story would be the least easy to explain?
    A   why Joe Clear sweated when he spent part of the night in a chair
    B   why there was a shortage of boarding house vacancies
    C   how the bedclothes had become ruffled
    D   how the bedroom door became locked

2. When Joe Clear went to the door after waking up for the first time he
    A   was experiencing hunger pains   B   wanted to see if it was locked
    C   was looking for a stranger   D   had decided to vacate the room

3. Which word best applies to Joe Clear's experience in the boarding house?
    A   gruesome   B   eerie   C   farcical   D   humiliating

4. How did the narrator react to his father's story?
    A   He regarded it as a factual recount of the event.
    B   He could not believe any of it.
    C   He thought it was repeated to upset him.
    D   He suspected parts of it might be true.

5. Which words from the text are an example of a metaphor?
    A   In he went and was met by a grey-faced woman
    B   a VACANT sign stuck out to fish in customers
    C   he had caught from her a strange smell of leaves
    D   sweating, he spent the night in a chair

6. What did Joe Clear find unusual about the woman running the boarding house?
    A   her calm response to his complaint   B   the grey colour of her face
    C   the speed she responded to his calls D   her earthy smell

7. Which word best describes Joe Clear's reaction to the door being locked a second time?
    A   cautious   B   irrational   C   enlightened   D   cunning

8. What was the first thing Joe Clear did when he initially woke up?

    A   he jumped out of bed   B   he began shouting
    C   he lit a candle   D   he checked to see who was on his bed

---

Lit Tip 29 – Improve your Literacy skills   **Word connotations**

Words often invoke a variety of responses in readers.
We usually think of moon in a very literal sense but it can have other connotations.
Blue moon - refers to a rare event (or whenever there are two full moons in a calendar month).
Blood moon - refers to a series of lunar eclipses. Over the moon - very excited, thrilled.
Moonshine - illicitly distilled alcohol in the US.   Honeymoon - a holiday after marriage.
Harvest moon - a full moon at the equinox, about when the harvest begins.
Research (You may use research sources.)
Find the meaning of: moonstruck _____

What is a moon-bow? _____

Angkor Wat

Built between roughly A.D. 1113 and 1150, and encompassing an area of about 200 hectares, Angkor Wat is one of the largest religious monuments ever constructed. Its name means "temple city". According to a 13th century Chinese traveller, it was believed by some that the temple was constructed in a single night by a divine architect.

The builder of Angkor Wat was a king named Suryavarman II. A usurper, he came to power in his teenage years by killing his great uncle, Dharanindravarman I, while the uncle was riding an elephant. An inscription says that Suryavarman killed the man "as Garuda (a mythical bird) on a mountain ledge would kill a serpent."

Originally built as a Hindu temple dedicated to the god Vishnu, it was converted into a Buddhist temple in the 13th Century. In the 14th century statues of Buddha were added to its already rich artwork.

Its 65 m central tower is surrounded by four smaller towers and a series of enclosure walls. This layout recreates the image of Mount Meru, a legendary place in Hindu mythology that is said to lie beyond the Himalayas and the home of the gods.

Angkor Wat Photo A. Horsfield

The city where the temple was built, Angkor, is located in modern-day Cambodia and was once the capital of the Khmer Empire. This city contains hundreds of temples. The population may have been over one million people.

Angkor contained an urban core that could have held 500,000 people with a vast hinterland that could have held many more inhabitants. Researchers have also identified the lost city called Mahendraparvata, which is located about 40 km north of Angkor Wat.

Angkor Wat itself is surrounded by a 200 m moat that encompasses a perimeter of more than 5 km. This moat is 4 m deep and would have helped stabilize the temple's foundation, preventing groundwater from rising too high or falling too low.

Building Angkor Wat was an enormous undertaking that involved quarrying, careful artistic work and lots of digging. To create the moat around the temple, 1.5 million cubic metres of sand and silt were moved, a task that would have required thousands of people working at one time.

A French explorer said that the temples were grander than anything built by Greece or Rome.

Sources: http://www.livescience.com/23841-angkor-wat.html
http://en.wikipedia.org/wiki/Angkor_Wat
Brochures available on the site

Understanding Reports

Circle a letter or write an answer for questions 1 to 8.

1. The general consensus over centuries is that Angkor Wat was a building of

    A   delicate intricacies   B   regal grandeur

    C   impressive proportions   D   pretentious displays

2. Who is believed to be the driving force behind the building of Angkor Wat?

    A   Vishnu   B   Dharanindravarman I

    C   Mahendraparvata   D   Suryavarman II

3. The *usurper* (paragraph 2) referred to in the passage was a person who

    A   took power by force   B   was next in line to be ruler

    C   constructed grand temples   D   rode elephants

4. According to the text what was the purpose of the moat around Angkor Wat?

    A   to create an aesthetic element suited to a fine temple

    B   to make the earth less susceptible to changes in groundwater levels

    C   to protect the building from invaders or intruders

    D   to provide a water supply for a huge city population

5. According to the text which statement is CORRECT?

    A   Angkor Wat was built in a single night by a divine architect.

    B   Angkor is one of several ancient cities in the region.

    C   The original Angkor buildings were the work of Buddhists.

    D   The ancient city of Angkor had a population of about 1000 people.

6. How long is the moat that surrounds Angkor Wat?

    A   200 metres   B   4 kilometres

    C   5 kilometres   D   40 kilometres

7. According to the text which statement is a FACT about Mount Meru?

    A   Mount Meru does not exist.   C   Mount Meru is in the Himalayas.

    B   Mount Meru is in Cambodia.   D   Mount Meru is important to Buddhism.

8. Which word from the text is a compound word?

    A   encompassing   B   hinterland   C   monuments   D   groundwater

---

Lit Tip 30 – Improve your Literacy skills   **Noun-verb agreement for quantities**

Expressions of time, money and measurements usually take a singular verb even though they appear to be plural nouns. (Check out Lit **Tip 13**.)

Amounts such as 2 litres, 3 minutes, $5, 4 kilometres, 40°C, 50 km/h, 2 tonnes take singular verbs.

Example: $6 is too much **NOT** $6 are too much.

Measurements are treated as single units.

Underline the correct verb.

    Ten minutes (is are) a long time to wait.

    Forty dollars (was were) lost on the train.

    Two litres of milk (remain remains) in the fridge.

    Fifteen dollars (seem seems) too much to pay.

    Two kilograms (have has) been taken from the case.

Understanding Year 7 Comprehension
A. Horsfield © Five Senses Education © W. Marlin

Read the information on *Book Covers*.

Book Covers

The Rats of Wolfe Island

Back cover text: It's an eerie mystery for Eddie Haite, whose casual summer holiday on a remote tropical island in Fiji, changes from an idyllic escape into a nightmare. Eddie, on a chance meeting, agrees to help a scientist, Rex King, carry out experiments on rats recovered from an old Pacific atomic testing site. As Eddie watches Rex descend into madness he realises there is something terrifying about the rats' strange behaviour.

Monopillar

Back cover text: From the time Jason boards the monorail from the Powerhouse Museum, he finds himself caught up in a creepy-crawly mystery that is out of this world. Who are the mysterious scientists watching his every move? Why are they carrying bags of bones around? And why is the monorail train starting to take on life-like features?

The Green Ambulance Caper

Back cover text: Tiffany discovers there is an ambulance for plants. She gets involved in plant rescues before coming across Nettle and Thistle, the Topiary twins, who have got a reputation for being harmful to plants. Investigations reveal even more. The Topiary twins have a scheme for releasing weeds into gardens and then being paid to remove them. The Topiary twins also put plants under stress by growing them espalier fashion.

Cadaver Dog

Back cover text: ' . . .Yeah, you should get yourself a dog. Never know when you will need one. Around here. Can't trust strangers.' There is something very disturbing about Clarry Johnson and his teenage daughter, Ellie, who daily pushes a pram up and down a dirt road. Shane's father has bought the old bush school next to Clarry's neglected orchard. It is an eerie place and it has a grim history that only Shane's dog, Caddy, can solve.

The Great Hair Robbery

Back cover text: Children have lost their hair. All adults have lost their hair, even the police. Santa Claus has lost his hair and Christmas looks like becoming a disaster. Nellie must solve the mystery with the aid of two bumbling detectives.

Understanding Book Covers

Circle a letter to answer questions 1 to 8.

1. What word best describes the genre of *Cadaver Dog*? (Check out Lit Tip 22.)
   A comedy
   B adventure
   C mystery
   D detective fiction

2. Which one of these books would most likely appeal to a younger reader?
   A *The Rats of Wolfe Island*
   B *The Great Hair Robbery*
   C *Monopillar*
   D *Cadaver Dog*

3. Which of the book covers suggests that the characters involved are in a cheerful adventure?
   A *The Great Hair Robbery*
   B *Monopillar*
   C *The Rats of Wolfe Island*
   D *The Green Ambulance Caper*

4. In which book is Eddie the main character?
   A *The Great Hair Robbery*
   B *Monopillar*
   C *The Rats of Wolfe Island*
   D *The Green Ambulance Caper*

5. Caddy is a cadaver dog in *Cadaver Dog*?
   Specifically, a cadaver dog is a dog that
   A has the ability to find human corpses
   B is trained to protect its owner
   C is bred to be a hunting dog
   D has been used in airport security

6. What is meant by the word *idyllic* as used in the text for *The Rats of Wolfe Island*?
   A idle and without useful employment
   B isolated or uncivilized
   C lacking purpose or direction
   D extremely pleasant and peaceful

7. The text on the back cover of *Monopillar* is a (Check out Lit Tip 31.)
   A blurb
   B review
   C summary
   D synopsis

8. The text on the back of a book is mostly intended
   A to provide reasons for publishing the book
   B to explain the graphics on the front cover
   C for promotional purposes
   D to pre-empt queries a buyer may have

Lit Tip 31 – Improve your Literacy skills   **Know the difference**

A **blurb** is a short positive description of a book to encourage sales of the book.
A **review** is a critical appraisal or rating of a book to inform buyers of a book's quality.
A **summary** is a brief statement about the main points in a book.
A **synopsis** is an outline of the plot of a book (or play or film).
In **your** opinion which book has the most successful blurb? (underline one)
The Rats of Wolfe Island   *Monopillar*   *The Green Ambulance Caper*
          The Great Hair Robbery   *Cadaver Dog*
Which literary device has the writer of the back cover text of *Monopillar* used to interest a potential buyer? (Circle a letter.)
A humour   B rhetorical questions   C unusual words   D an explanation

Understanding Year 7 Comprehension
A. Horsfield © Five Senses Education © W. Marlin

Historic Houses

Kemp House and the Stone Store are two of New Zealand's oldest buildings and are situated in the Kerikeri Basin. Kemp House and the Stone Store are the only survivors from the Church Missionary Society's (CMS) second Anglican mission to New Zealand, founded in 1819 on land granted to the Reverend Samuel Marsden by the powerful Nga Puhi (Maori) chief, Hongi Hika. Kemp House is the oldest surviving European building in New Zealand. The Stone Store is the country's oldest surviving stone building.

The Stone Store was built in 1832-36 as a storehouse for the mission.	The nearby Kemp House was built by the Reverend John Gare Butler in 1821-22 as a mission house.
Stone Store (left, above the water)	Kemp House (right, above the lawn)

From 1824 - 1831 Kemp House was occupied by the lay missionary George Clarke and from mid - 1832 by blacksmith and lay missionary James Kemp and his family. The mission was closed in 1848, but the Kemps stayed on, eventually buying the house from the CMS. Their descendants lived there until 1974 when Ernest Kemp presented the house and its contents to the New Zealand Historic Places Trust.

After the mission's closure the Stone Store was taken over by the Kemp family and leased by a succession of storekeepers. In 1976 the New Zealand Historic Places Trust, which continued to operate it as a shop, bought it from the A.E. Kemp Estate. The building has had major conservation and renovation work and reopened for the public during 1998.

The Stone Store was constructed to hold mission supplies and wheat from the mission farm at Te Waimate, but the building was mainly leased as a kauri (NZ tree) gum-trading store. Today, you can shop for authentic frontier trade goods and tourist souvenirs.

The Stone Store as a Post Office

Sources: http://www.kerikeri.co.nz/Kemp_House_and_Stone_Store.cfm
http://www.kerikeri.co.nz/The_Stone_Store.cfm
On-site information

Understanding Recounts

Circle a letter or write an answer for questions 1 to 8.

1. The land for the Reverend Samuel Marsden's mission was a grant from
   A   Nga Puhi (Maori) chief, Hongi Hika
   B   Church Missionary Society
   C   the A.E. Kemp Estate
   D   New Zealand Historic Places Trust

2. Kemp House was built more recently than the Stone Store. Is this TRUE or FALSE?

   Tick a box.   TRUE ☐   FALSE ☐

3. Who presented the house and contents to the New Zealand Historic Places Trust?
   A   George Clarke   B   Ernest Kemp
   C   James Kemp   D   Rev. Samuel Marsden

4. Write the numbers 1 to 4 in the boxes to show the correct order in which events occurred in the recount.

   ☐ Stone Store building commenced
   ☐ New Zealand Historic Places Trust buys Kemp House
   ☐ Anglican Mission founded in New Zealand
   ☐ James Kemp occupies Kemp House

5. George Clarke was a lay missionary. A *lay missionary* is one who
   A   is **not** ordained but is permitted to spread the gospel
   B   is recognised for his knowledge of local customs
   C   can lay down the laws that are part of a church's teaching
   D   belongs to a group of missionaries trained for foreign service

6. Which group or organisation had the longest occupancy of Kemp House?
   A   the Church Missionary Society
   B   Nga Puhi (Maori) chief, Hongi Hika
   C   New Zealand Historic Places Trust
   D   successive generations of the Kemp families

7. The stone building is described as a store. *Store* in the original context meant a
   A   place where goods were sold   B   display area of saleable goods
   C   building where produce was kept   D   shed for army equipment

8. Who was responsible for the building of Kemp House?
   A   George Clarke   B   James Kemp
   C   Rev. John Gare Butler   D   Rev. Samuel Marsden

Lit Tip 32 – Improve your Literacy skills   **Adjective types**

In high school you will become more precise in your understanding of grammar.
Here are some adjective types (underlined):
Numbering: Jim has <u>five</u> books.
Descriptive: It was a <u>grey</u> morning for a <u>bush</u> walk.
Demonstrative: Did you see <u>those</u> bikies yesterday?
Proper: The <u>French</u> soldiers lost the battle.
Underline the adjectives in this sentence.

| **Other examples** |
| fourth, twenty |
| safe, old |
| that, this |
| Martian, Shakespearean |

In the third quarter the junior African players replaced their dirty boots for bare feet!

Understanding Year 7 Comprehension
A. Horsfield © Five Senses Education © W. Marlin

Make a Seismometer

A seismometer or seismograph is an instrument used by scientists to measure and record the strength and duration of earthquakes and tremors. It works on a simple pendulum principal. A weight (a bob) hangs on a string which can swing.

When the ground shakes, the base and frame of the instrument move with it, but the pendulum bob stays in one place. It will then appear to move, relative to the shaking ground. As it moves it records the pendulum displacements as they change with time, tracing out a record called a seismogram.

You Will Need:

Cornflakes box (or similar)   Sand
Plastic cup with cover   Pencil
Scissors   Piece of string
Cardboard sheet (size of cornflakes box)
Strip of paper (3cm wide, by 50cm long)

A seismogram

Small stick

Steps

1. Cut a rectangle out of both sides of a cornflakes box, leaving a 3cm wide border.

2. Cut two narrow horizontal slots near the base of the box about 3cm wide through which you can slide your strip of paper (as shown).

3. Pierce small holes in the centre of the cup cover and in the bottom of the cup.

4. Push a pencil, point down, through the two holes. Half-fill the cup with sand around the pencil. Reposition the lid.

5. You may have to thread string through the holes near the top of opposite sides of the cup to stop the cup from sliding down.

6. Hang the cup from the centre of the cereal box tied to a small stick on the box top (see diagram).

7. Adjust the length of the string. The pencil lead should just touch the strip of paper threaded through the bottom slots of the box.

8. Glue the bottom of the cornflakes box to one of the sheets of cardboard.

Test Run

Gently shake the cardboard base back and forth. Have an assistant slowly___(5)___the strip of paper through the slits. The weighted pencil should stay put and mark the paper strip, seismometer fashion, as it comes through the slits.

Adapted from: http://www.kfvs12.com/Global/story.asp?S=307729&nav=LuIGLi2z

Understanding Procedures

Circle a letter or write an answer for questions 1 to 8.

1. The seismometer described in these instructions would be most useful
   A in outdoor settings
   B for amateur scientists
   C for rescue agencies
   D in science laboratories

2. The two slits cut into the cornflakes box, near its base are to
   A let the bob swing freely
   B keep the pencil from marking the base of the frame
   C provide a sight line for lining up the parts of the seismometer
   D guide the strip of paper along a fixed route

3. As used in the text the words *stays in one place* could be replaced with
   A remains stationary
   B is immobilised
   C becomes inanimate
   D is at a standstill

4. The purpose of the small stick on the top of the cornflakes box is to
   A stabilise the cornflakes box
   B reinforce the weakened structure
   C prevent the string from slipping through the hole
   D secure the pencil to the string

5. A word has been deleted from the text.
   Which word would be best suited to the space (5)?
   A draw
   B push
   C steer
   D direct

6. You may need an assistant to test your seismometer.
   What does the assistant have to do?
   A hold pieces of construction in place while other parts are being made
   B pull the paper strip though the slits when the seismometer is shaken
   C gently shake the seismometer to check its sturdiness
   D provide items required in construction that are not readily available

7. Which step is most likely an optional step?
   A Step 3
   B Step 4
   C Step 5
   D Step 6

8. Write the numbers 1 to 4 in the boxes to show the order in which steps are taken to make the seismometer.

	adjust the length of string holding the pencil
	remove the two opposite sides from a cornflakes box
	half fill the plastic cup with sand
	force a pencil, point down, through holes on a covered plastic cup

---

Lit Tip 33 – Improve your Literacy skills   **Colons**

Colons (:) are a form of punctuation.
They indicate a pause and more information will follow.
Examples of colon use
Take care to include these essentials: water, matches, sunscreen and a hat. (Lists)
Linda had two hates: football and big dogs.
Note: In the first two examples the colon follows a complete sentence.
Paris to London: The Great Race. (Book title from its subtitle)
8:45 (between hours and minutes)
Jack: Where are you going Jill? (Play scripts) Now write the reply Jill might make.

_____

Understanding Year 7 Comprehension
A. Horsfield © Five Senses Education © W. Marlin

34 Read the explanation *How a Canyon is Formed.*

How a Canyon is Formed

A canyon or gorge is a deep ravine between a pair of cliffs or escarpments often carved from the landscape by a river. Rivers have a tendency to cut through underlying surfaces and wear away and expose successive rock layers. This forms a canyon.

Carnarvon Gorge Qld. Photo A. Horsfield

Most canyons were formed by long-time erosion from a plateau (a high plain). The floor of a canyon is often very narrow unlike the sweep of valleys of the western slopes of NSW where rain is more prevalent.

The word canyon is Spanish in origin (cañón) and is generally used in the USA while the word gorge is more common in Europe and Australia (e.g. Carnarvon Gorge, Qld) though gorge, ravine and gulch are also used in some parts of the USA and Canada.

Canyons are much more common in arid areas than in wet areas because physical weathering has a greater effect in arid zones. The wind and water from the river combine to erode and cut away less resistant rock. The freezing and expansion of water also serves to help form canyons. Water seeps into cracks between the rocks and freezes, pushing the rocks apart and eventually causing large blocks to break off the canyon walls, in a process known as frost wedging. Water when it freezes expands. Submarine canyons form underwater, generally at the mouths of rivers.

Sometimes large rivers run through canyons as the result of gradual geological uplift. These are called entrenched rivers, because they are less able to easily alter their course, such as the Colorado River in the Grand Canyon (Arizona, USA).

Mossman Gorge Qld Photo A. Horsfield

Canyons can form in areas of limestone rock. Limestone tends to be soluble, so cave systems form in the rock. When these collapse a canyon is left. A canyon may result from a rift (blocks of the earth's surface plates separating) between two mountain peaks in ranges such as the Rocky Mountains (N. America), the Alps (Europe), the Himalayas (northern India) or the Andes (S. America). Usually rivers carve out such splits between mountains but other forces may be involved. Gorges that only have an opening on one end are called box canyons. Slot canyons are very____ (3) canyons, often with smooth walls.

Adapted from: http://en.wikipedia.org/wiki/Canyon

Understanding Explanations

Circle a letter to answer questions 1 to 8.

1. Valleys differ from canyons in that canyons are
   - A   longer than valleys
   - B   more common in wetter regions
   - C   more accessible than valleys
   - D   narrower than valleys

2. It is most likely canyons are less common in areas of high rainfall because
   - A   they have greater vegetation cover slowing down erosion processes
   - B   the layers of rock in the canyon walls are harder
   - C   the wind has little influence in high rainfall areas
   - D   there are less limestone areas in wet regions

3. A word has been deleted from the text.
   Which word would be best suited to the space (3)?
   - A   narrow
   - B   high
   - C   rugged
   - D   harsh

4. In what way does water freezing contribute to the formation of canyons?
   - A   It solidifies the base of insecure cliff rocks.
   - B   It forms a hard surface on softer rock making it brittle.
   - C   It combines with loose rubble to be washed away.
   - D   It expands then forces the rocks to break from cliffs as the water freezes.

5. What feature does the arrow point to in this sketch?
   - A   a gulch
   - B   an escarpment
   - C   a box canyon
   - D   an entrenched river

6. According to the text which statement is CORRECT?
   - A   Canyons cannot form under the ocean.
   - B   Canyons regularly change the course of rivers.
   - C   Canyons are the result of various forms of erosion.
   - D   Canyons are no longer forming on Earth.

7. Which word from the text goes least with the other three?
   - A   ravine
   - B   plateau
   - C   gorge
   - D   gulch

8. The information *How a Canyon is Formed* would most likely be found in a junior reference material on
   - A   biology
   - B   meteorology
   - C   astrology
   - D   geology

Lit Tip 34 – Improve your Literacy skills   **Comparing adjectives**

Adjectives can show different degrees of the quality they are describing.
Comparative adjectives compare two items: My apple is red*der* than yours.
Superlative adjectives compare more than two items: My apple is the red*dest* of all.
This pattern of *er* and *est* is common with adjectives: hot, hot*ter*, hot*test*
However some adjectives are **irregular!** Look at: good, better, best

Can you complete this table?

bad	worse	?
little	less	
many/much	?	most
far	farther	?

For distance:

Understanding Year 7 Comprehension
A. Horsfield © Five Senses Education © W. Marlin

Read the explanation for riding *Segways* *(Personal Mobility Devices).*

Segways

A personal mobility device (PMD or segway) can be used on footpaths, bike paths and shared pathways. PMDs must comply with the following conditions:

☐ Be designed for use by a single person (no passenger).

☐ Be self-balancing (while in use).

☐ Be powered by an electric motor.

☐ Have 2 wheels that operate on a single axis.

☐ Have a maximum speed of 20 km/h.

☐ Have a control to limit speed to 12 km/h or less.

☐ Have a maximum width of 85 cm.

Rules for Using a Segway

A range of conditions apply to the use of approved PMDs on pathways. People caught not following these conditions will be fined.

✓ be aged 16 and over to operate a PMD unsupervised
✓ be supervised by an adult if aged between 12 and 15
✓ wear a bicycle helmet that is securely fitted
✓ keep left when travelling on a pathway
✓ give way to pedestrians on a pathway
✓ keep left to oncoming bicycles on a path
✓ have a warning bell or horn
✓ have a working flashing or steady white light at the front, a red light and a red reflector at the rear to use at night or in hazardous conditions

PERSONAL MOBILITY DEVICES PROHIBITED

A Segway Operator Must Not:

* travel faster than 12 km/hour
* travel along a road unless there is an obstruction or it is impractical
* carry passengers
* use a hand-held mobile phone
* drink alcohol while operating a segway
* travel past a 'PMD prohibited' sign

(Note: PMD users may remain on their device to cross a road at a designated crossing.)

Local councils and landowners can prohibit segways in areas not appropriate for their use, such as malls, esplanades or jetties. A 'PMD prohibited' sign will be displayed in such areas.

Adapted from: http://www.tmr.qld.gov.au/Safety/Queensland-road-rules/Personal-mobility-devices.aspx

Understanding Explanations

Circle a letter or write an answer for questions 1 to 8.

1. Segway operators are allowed to use public roads when they
   - A   encounter obstructions on shared footpaths
   - B   travel at speeds more than 12 km/h
   - C   use a devise powered by an electric motor
   - D   are carrying a passenger

2. In the section **Segways** you read: *PMDs must <u>comply with</u> the following conditions.*
   As used in the text which word could replace *comply with* without loss of meaning?
   - A   accept   B   observe   C   understand   D   remember

3. What is the meaning of *range* as used in the subsection **Rules for Using a Segway**?
   - A   a distant limitation   B   a line of mountains or hills
   - C   a set of restricting conditions   D   an area of land set aside for public use

4. A segway rider is permitted to
   - A   carry one passenger on shared pathways
   - B   ride unsupervised after the age of 12 years
   - C   travel up to of 20 km/h on roadways
   - D   stay on the device when crossing a road

5. On which side of a designated pathway should a segway be driven?
   Write your answer on the line. _____

6. It is most likely that the riding of segways is permitted
   - A   in shopping centres   B   along seaside walkways
   - C   on wharves and piers   D   on pedestrian crossings

7. A segway must be equipped with
   - A   traffic indicators   B   an audible warning device
   - C   restraining belts   D   passenger foot rests

8. What is the most likely reason for these PMD regulations?
   - A   to ensure the safety of both riders and pedestrians
   - B   to reduce the amount of traffic on public roads
   - C   to encourage people to consider PMDs as a mode of transport
   - D   to raise government funds through fines

Lit Tip 35 – Improve your Literacy skills   Apostrophes

Inverted commas are most often used around direct speech. (See **Lit Tip 16**.)
They can be doubles ("x") or singles ('x'). Singles are also used as apostrophes.
They can be used to show contractions (*I'm* for *I am*.)
They can be used to show missing letters most often in dialogue in narratives or plays.
Examples: Are *yercomin' 'ome* and *Where'yer get that 'at*?
Rewrite this sentence to include all the missing letters.
'Ey! 'Ow's 'arry goin' to get to 'ere if it's rainin'?

Understanding Year 7 Comprehension
A. Horsfield © Five Senses Education © W. Marlin

Understanding Cloud Symbols

Clouds are categorised and sorted into various types, based on their properties.

1. Layered or Stratiform clouds: Stratiform clouds appear in layers or strata. There are three levels in the troposphere (the lowest region of the atmosphere) where these types of clouds appear in different forms.
   - Stratus clouds form at the lowest levels.
   - Altostratus clouds form at the middle levels.
   - Cirrostratus clouds form at the highest levels. These have some properties of cirrus clouds and some properties of stratus clouds.

2. Puffy or Cumuliform clouds: Cumuliform clouds are the puffy, fair weather clouds that look like big balls of cotton. They can be found at all three levels of the atmosphere in different forms. Cumulus clouds form about 1.5 km up to about 3 km.
   - Altocumulus clouds can be found in the 3-6 km range.
   - Cirrocumulus clouds are found at the highest range.
   - Stratocumulus clouds have properties of both stratus and cumulus clouds. They are found in the higher portions of the lowest level.

3. Rain clouds: Clouds that produce rain contain the word nimbus in some form.
   - Nimbostratus clouds produce rain or snow. When it rains or snows all day it is generally from nimbostratus clouds.
   - Cumulonimbus clouds are formed when moist air from the low levels of the atmosphere is carried high into the troposphere. Cumulonimbus clouds are the thunderheads that produce thunderstorms and even tornadoes.

Weather conditions are reported on weather maps using symbols. The table below lists the symbols and the cloud names used when reporting weather.

Symbol	Cloud Name	Symbol	Cloud Name	Symbol	Cloud Name
—	Stratus	⌒	Cumulus	⌣	Stratocumulus
∠	Altostratus	ᴗ	Altocumulus	⟋	Nimbostratus
2	Cirrostratus	ᘔ	Cirrocumulus	⌂	Cumulonimbus

The clouds can also be grouped according to their altitude.

- High clouds include cirrus (wispy clouds), cirrostratus and cirrocumulus
- Middle level clouds include altostratus and altocumulus
- Low clouds include cumulus, stratus and stratocumulus
- Ground level clouds are called fog

Adapted from: http://www.kean.edu/~fosborne/resources/ex10g.htm

Understanding Explanations

Circle a letter to answer questions 1 to 8.

1. A cloud type that has nimbus as part of its name is a
   - A middle-level cloud
   - B fluffy cloud
   - C thin cloud
   - D rain bearing cloud

2. The cumuliform cloud are readily recognised by their
   - A colour
   - B appearance
   - C size
   - D altitude

3. Which cloud type is represented by this symbol?
   - A cirrostratus
   - B cumulus
   - C altocumulus
   - D cirrostratus

4. The cloud in this picture is most likely a?
   - A cumulonimbus
   - B cirrostratus
   - C altocumulus
   - D nimbostratus

5. You read in subsection **2** *fair weather clouds that look like big balls of cotton.*
   The term, *like big balls of cotton*, is an example of a
   - A metaphor
   - B hyperbole
   - C simile
   - D cliché (Check **Lit Tip 37.**)

6. Which cloud type may be associated with tornadoes?
   - A altostratus
   - B cumulonimbus
   - C cirrostratus
   - D stratocumulus

7. When the sky is filled with nimbostratus clouds it suggests that
   - A the sky will soon clear
   - B a storm is likely
   - C the skies will be bright
   - D it could rain all day

8. At which altitude would these wispy clouds be located?
   - A below 1.5 km
   - B high in the troposphere
   - C at ground level
   - D above the troposphere

Lit Tip 36 – Improve your Literacy skills   **Noun-verb agreement**

Singular nouns need singular verbs. Plural nouns need plural verbs. (See **Lit Tip 13.**)
Most plural nouns end with an s and most singular verbs end with an s.
There are many singular nouns that end with s: athletics, physics, billiards, darts, mathematics, measles, statistics. They have no plural form.
These nouns take singular verbs.
Example: Athletics requires sustained effort.
Underline the correct verb to complete these sentences.

1. The news (is are) bad.   **2.** Bowls (require requires) a strict dress code.
3. Mumps (cause causes) severe neck pains.   **4.** Aerobics (help helps) to keep you fit.

Understanding Year 7 Comprehension
A. Horsfield © Five Senses Education © W. Marlin

Clichés

Clichés in writing and in speech add little to what is being communicated. A cliché is an overused expression, for example, as old as the hills.

An overused expression is something that is said so often it no longer really has any value or is even noticed in conversation. Phrases such as, in deep water, is an example of such a cliché. People often say these phrases without noticing they are doing so.

A cliché is also an expression which carries a different meaning from its literal meaning. For example, the phrase, his head in the sand, does not mean someone has actually put their in the sand. That is the literal meaning. The intended meaning is that the person is ignoring something unpleasant as if it doesn't exist. Everyone knows this because the expression has become a cliché.

A cliché can be two things:

1. An overused expression, something that is said so often that it has become meaningless. It has little relevance or is even noticed in conversation. The phrase, this point in time is an example of such a cliché. You may often say it without noticing you are doing so.

2. An idea with a different meaning from the literal meaning. For example, the phrase twinkling eyes has come to mean more than your eye's have a twinkle.

In everyday writing clichés are often used as similes. They show a lack of originality on the part of the writer. Here are some very common ones:

    as brave as a lion   as black as pitch (tar)

They may be used as hyperboles (exaggeration).

    as fast as the speed of light   as old as the hills

Metaphors can be clichés. Here are some common ones:

    scared out of my wits   cat's got my tongue

    has nerves of steel   got out of the wrong side of the bed

Remember, clichés are too predictable and too familiar to be interesting. Using worn-out phrases suggests to the reader that you, the writer, have no imagination!

However, in general speech it is almost impossible not to rely on some worn-out phrases if we're to be understood quickly and precisely! Have your parents ever told you: money doesn't grow on trees?

Can you complete these very common clichés?

He painted himself into a _____

Don't get your knickers in a _____

It was as easy as _____

Don't beat around the _____

Birds of a feather flock _____

Suggested answers: corner, knot, pie, bush, together

Understanding Explanations

Circle a letter to answer questions 1 to 8.

1. Clichés are most commonly used in
   A   news reports
   B   official writing
   C   everyday conversations
   D   safety manuals

2. What does someone mean when they say they *are over the moon*?
   A   they are very excited and happy
   B   they are worried by heights
   C   they are exceptionally capable athletes
   D   they have grand ambitions

3. What is the intended meaning of the saying a *month of Sundays*?
   A   a period without work
   B   the last Sunday of the month
   C   a month of five Sundays
   D   a very long time

4. *As white as snow* and *as cold as ice* are examples of clichés used as
   A   metaphors   B   similes   C   euphemisms   D   slang

5. What is one advantage of using clichés?
   A   they make listeners consider what is being said
   B   they improve the quality of conversation
   C   their meaning can be quickly appreciated
   D   many people find them very amusing

6. A saying becomes a cliché when it is used
   A   by important people
   B   to hide personal feelings
   C   for it's literal meaning
   D   often without thought

7. What is the part of speech of the word *value* as used in Paragraph 2?
   A   verb   B   pronoun   C   adjective   D   noun

8. Which cliché best describes someone doing something silly or dangerous?
   A   playing with fire
   B   burning bridges
   C   fighting fire with fire
   D   burning a candle at both ends

Lit Tip 37 – Improve your Literacy skills   **More on clichés**

Draw a line to match the cliché with its intended meaning.

1. tail between his legs   A under fed
2. sweaty hands   B it will happen
3. bag of bones   C feeling nervous
4. writing on the wall   D very miserable

Tick the best meaning for:
at the drop of a hat
A very quickly
B being careless
C about to relax

Remember, clichés do not improve your writing.

Understanding Year 7 Comprehension
A. Horsfield © Five Senses Education © W. Marlin

The Gymnast

She is mercury gliding on a beam

like rhythm rolling

a coiled helix unwinding on a mat

she vaults the silent horse

spins somersaults

Sinew stretched and weaving air

she leaps star-wards

with concertina limbs

this curved comet orbits hovers

near the moon

Spirals, spirals and mocks gravity

certain of trajectory

and on re-entry she lands soft

on feather feet

platinum strong

and arrow straight

Sheryl Persson

My thanks to Sheryl Persson for permission to reproduce this poem.

Understanding Poetry

Circle a letter or write an answer for questions 1 to 8.

1. In the first line of the poem, the poet is suggesting that the gymnast is
   A   clever   B   supple   C   healthy   D   robust

2. Complete the sentence by writing your answer on the line.
   (**Note:** Several possible answers.)
   If you are on a certain *trajectory*, you are following a particular _____.

3. Which two words from the poem are most similar in meaning?
   A   *vaults* and *spins*
   B   *unwinding* and *weaving*
   C   *hovers* and *floats*
   D   *stretched* and *strong*

4. Which quotation from the poem is an example of a simile?
   A   'like rhythm rolling'   B   'with concertina limbs'
   C   'near the moon'   D   'on feather feet'

5. In the lines 'she vaults the silent horse / spins somersaults' the poet uses
   A   personification to highlight physical actions
   B   metaphor to create the sense of touch
   C   onomatopoeia to describe the apparatus
   D   alliteration to appeal to the sense of sound

6. The poet draws on imagery from all of the following fields except
   A   astronomy   B   archery
   C   metals   D   medicine

7. In the last stanza the word 'spirals' is used as
   A   a noun   B   an adjective   C   a verb   D   an adverb

8. You can conclude from the poem that the poet
   A   is worried that the gymnast will be injured
   B   admires the remarkable skill of the gymnast
   C   believes the gymnast will win competitions
   D   is impressed by the gymnast's commitment to training

Lit Tip 38 – Improve your Literacy skills   **Improving narratives 3**

Often in narratives writers focus on what can be seen. (Check out **Lit Tip 25** and **26**.)
It is important in narratives (and descriptions) to include text that focuses on other senses. What sense does this text focus on?
Joanne was still peckish. She continued to sit at the breakfast bar looking at the burnt toast spread with butter and sickly, sweet honey. What would she give for something a little bit savoury. Maybe a mouth-watering bite of a spicy hamburger with the tang of Spanish onions*.
Write your answer on the line. _____

(* adapted from Creative Writing Years 5 / 6 A. Horsfield Excel 2004)

Understanding Year 7 Comprehension
A. Horsfield © Five Senses Education © W. Marlin

Floods, Drought and the Southern Oscillation Index*

(*scale)

There are two main atmospheric circulations responsible for causing droughts and floods in Australia. These are El Niño and La Nina events.

El Niño is part of the Southern Oscillation, which is a huge climatic pattern that covers the Pacific Ocean and influences the weather in Australia. In a normal pattern, easterly winds flow across the Pacific (the south-easterly trades), bringing moisture and driving warm ocean currents onto the Australian coast. These winds then rise over northern Australia and condense to give rain. If the trade winds are strong there are likely to be floods and tropical cyclones.

About every five years the whole pattern is disturbed. In an El Niño year, the water off the South American coast becomes warmer as the rising up of cold water stops. This change creates lower than normal air pressure which weakens the trade winds, or can reverse them. Without trade winds to drive the circulating current it reverses, causing a 'wave' of warm water to surge eastward rather than west. With little wind picking up moisture from the cooler-than-usual sea, there is less rainfall over eastern Australia.

La Nina is the opposite of El Niño. During La Nina the seas north of Australia become slightly warmer while the eastern Pacific Ocean becomes considerably cooler. This intensifies the easterly trade winds which pick up more moisture from the warm water. The result is often above-average rainfall over much of the eastern coast of Australia.

Meteorologists have been able to determine that pressure changes can be used to predict changing weather patterns and have developed a system known as the Southern Oscillation Index (SOI). SOI is calculated from the monthly or seasonal fluctuations in the air pressure difference between Tahiti and Darwin.

El Niño events follow an annual pattern developing in autumn, holding through winter, spring and summer, and then either breaking down or re-establishing in the autumn of the following year. Likewise SOI is usually set by the end of May and this phase can be used to indicate rainfall patterns over the next nine months - until the start of the next autumn. Positive readings in autumn usually mean above average rainfall and negative readings usually mean lower than average rainfall.

For farmers the SOI is a useful tool but it is only an indication of higher or lower than average rainfall, not rainfall amounts.

Sources: http://www.bom.gov.au/climate/glossary/soi.shtml http://www.tocal.nsw.edu.au/farms/Tocals-e-farm/the-climate-of-tocal/floods,-drought-and-the-southern-oscillation-index

http://www.weatherzone.com.au/climate/indicator_enso.jsp?c=soi

Understanding Explanations   Circle a letter or write an answer for questions 1 to 8.

1. What is the meaning of *oscillation* in the name **Southern Oscillation Index**?
   - A   a movement back and forth
   - B   an unpredictable fluctuation
   - C   an irregular rotation
   - D   a violent swinging between extremes

2. In the first paragraph the writer refers to *atmospheric circulations*.
   These are circulations of
   - A   ocean currents
   - B   air pressure cells
   - C   yearly seasonal changes
   - D   wind movements

3. An El Niño event mainly originates in the
   - A   Southern Ocean
   - B   Pacific Ocean
   - C   Indian Ocean
   - D   Antarctic Ocean

4. Write the numbers 1 to 4 in the boxes to show the correct order in which El Niño events develop.

warm ocean currents are driven onto the Australian coast
the south-east trades blow across the Pacific Ocean
strong winds follow that may cause flooding or cyclones
winds rise off the Australian landform and produce rain

5. According to the text which statement is CORRECT?
   - A   The Southern Oscillation Index is used to calculate rainfall totals.
   - B   Cool Pacific Ocean currents cause winds to blow towards South America.
   - C   The Southern Oscillation Index is usually consistent for at least four years.
   - D   During a La Nina event the seas north of Australia become slightly cooler.

6. Which community group is mostly likely to be very interested in changes in the SOI?

   Write your answer on the line. _____

7. In which season is a new El Niño pattern most likely to begin to develop?
   - A   autumn   B   summer   C   winter   D   spring

8. Positive El Niño readings of the SOI in autumn usually mean
   - A   that cyclones are unlikely
   - B   lower Pacific Ocean temperatures
   - C   on shore winds will cease
   - D   above average rainfall in Australia

Lit Tip 39 – Improve your Literacy skills   Know the differences (names)

People often have a name other than their given name.
An **alias** is used to indicate that a named person is also known by a more familiar name. It often has criminal connotations.
A **pen** name (or **nom de plume** or **pseudonym**) is a name used by a writer instead of their real name.
A **stage name** is a name used by an actor instead of their real name.
A **nickname** is a humorous name given to a person in place of their real name.
What are these names examples of?
A man with red hair is called Bluey. _____
Mark Twain's (wrote *Huckleberry Finn*) real name was Samuel Clemens. _____

Understanding Year 7 Comprehension
A. Horsfield © Five Senses Education © W. Marlin

After the Chase

Blake lay on his bed in the semi-darkness. He was safe - for the moment, at least.

His thoughts drifted to his first meeting with Brooke and almost laughed out aloud. Brooke, what a crazy way to name a girl he thought. But then there were sillier names. Phoenix and Bambi came quickly to mind. Unconsciously he rubbed his flabby belly.

Downstairs he could sense his mother getting things ready for the evening meal. Her thoughts were vague and gentle. He guessed she might be singing, or humming, to herself. Maybe she had the radio on one of those 'soft and easy hits' channels.

His father was probably in the shed fixing something, or painting something, or repairing something someone had given to him. Or, just as likely, it was something he had found. Blake often felt his father was an embarrassment.

Then his mind went back to the chase. They probably wouldn't have hurt him. They just needed to get the evidence. He shivered involuntarily.

Chiciac. The chicken. He was all right. He was a bit scrawny like an underfed rooster. Would he do anything without the others? Probably not. But he would be happy to join in given a bit of encouragement. Blake suddenly sniggered. Chickenman's snout was even like a chook's beak. Blake could just imagine him covered with feathers and becoming some comic superhero, Chickenman. Or, as an alternative, being almost featherless and embarrassed. The naked Chicken strikes again!!

Then there was Kevin. Now Kevin was a bit different. Kevin was a teaser. He would annoy until someone lost his, or her, temper then he would walk off innocently.

"I don't know what happened," he would say. "Got nothing to do with me. I was just walking past and suddenly he does his 'nana. Didn't see anything." All innocence. Everyone knew it was not like that at all. Except the adults - and especially the teachers.

But Brad. . . Brad was mean. He thought everyone was out to get him. Who'd bother? But Brad believed they would. He would do things openly. He'd thump someone, anytime, if he felt crossed. Brad could bear a grudge, harbour a hate for as long as it took for him to get revenge. He must spend more time feeling mad than he does feeling good, thought Blake. Blake could sense his bad vibes just by being nearby. He was full of angry energy.

"And thinking of energy", Blake mused to himself, "I need to get fit." Then he added with a soft laugh, "But I don't have the energy."

Understanding Narratives

Circle a letter to answer questions 1 to 8.

1. What is the most likely reason Blake was lying on his bed?
    A   he was recovering after being chased
    B   he was hiding from his pursuers
    C   he was waiting to be called for a meal
    D   he was avoiding helping his father in the shed

2. Blake could best be described as
    A   indolent and suspicious
    B   unmotivated and reflective
    C   brooding and anxious
    D   careless and agitated

3. Which literary genre would be most applicable for this text? (Check out **Lit Tip 22**.)
    A   science fiction   B   romance   C   adventure   D   humour

4. Blake's last musing (final paragraph) contains an example of
    A   a metaphor
    B   idiomatic speech
    C   a hyperbole
    D   an ironic situation (Check out **Lit Tip 17**.)

5. In which order did Blake experience these events?
    1. he thought about Brook
    2. he was chased by three people
    3. he takes refuge in his bedroom
    4. he listened to his mother working
    A   **2, 4, 1, 3**   B   **3, 4, 2, 1**   C   **2, 3, 1, 4**   D   **1, 2, 3, 4**

6. *His father was probably in the shed fixing <u>something</u>.* (paragraph 4)
    What part of speech is something in this context?
    A   noun   B   adverb   C   adjective   D   pronoun

7. Which character amongst Blake's contacts did he take most delight in mocking?
    A   Brook   B   Chiciac   C   Kevin   D   Brad

8. The second last paragraph begins with: *But Brad . . .*
    The ellipsis (. . .) is used to indicate (Check out **Lit Tip 27**.)
    A   a momentary pause in Blake's thinking
    B   that Blake is drifting off to sleep
    C   a word has been omitted from the text
    D   that Blake is having difficulties keeping focused

Lit Tip 40 – Improve your Literacy skills　　　　　**The prefix *be***

The prefix *be* can change the meaning of a base word.
It can express an action (verbs): *befriend, besiege, bedazzle*
It can be added to nouns and verbs: *befool, befriend*
It can have the meaning of all over or thoroughly: *bespatter, bewilder, bedazzle*

1. Which be word means:
A. cut off the head _____   B. to be loved _____
C. a late birthday wish is a _____ wish

2. Which be expression has the meaning of 'go away!? _____

Understanding Year 7 Comprehension
A. Horsfield © Five Senses Education © W. Marlin

SOLUTIONS

Understanding Year 7 Comprehension
A. Horsfield © Five Senses Education © W. Marlin

Answers

Year 7 Comprehension Questions

No.	Title	Answers

1. Deep Beyond the Reef: 1. C   2. A   3. D   4. A   5. B   6. C   7. B   8. D

2. Green Ants in North QLD: 1. B   2. C   3. A   4. D   5. A   6. C   7. D   8. 8 years

3. Bosley: 1. B   2. D   3. A   4. B   5. C   6. D   7. A   8. C

4. The Earthquake: 1. B   2. D   3. C   4. A   5. A   6. D   7. B   8. A

5. Canning Stock Route: 1. D   2. 37   3. Halls Creek - Wiluna   4. B   5. (4, 2, 3, 1)   6. A   7. C   8. D

6. Gumleaf Playing: 1. A   2. B   3. D   4. A   5. C   6. B   7. C   8. D

7. Terms for Dying: 1. D   2. B   3. A   4. C   5. B   6. C   7. D   8. A

8. Great Fire of London: 1. D   2. B   3. C   4. A   5. wind died down   6. C   7. A   8. D

9. Elimination Tournaments: 1. A   2. 3   3. B   4. D   5. C   6. Lyn   7. A   8. D

10. Pigeon Houses of France: 1. TRUE   2. D   3. B   4. C   5. A   6. B   7. C   8. D

11. Tidy Town Scheme: 1. B   2. C   3. A   4. D   5. high visibility   6. D   7. A   8. D

12. Book Review - Kangaroo: 1. C   2. D   3. B   4. C   5. A   6. Reds / Greys   7. A   8. D

13. Meanings Change: 1. B   2. C   3. 1710   4. A   5. D   6. C   7. D   8. A

14. The Brook: 1. A   2. B   3. A   4. C   5. D   6. B   7. D   8. C

15. Playing Dominoes: 1. C   2. D   3. A   4. B   5. C   6. D   7. B   8. A

16. Pulp Fiction: 1. B   2. C   3. B   4. A   5. D   6. C   7. A   8. D

17. Lake Taupo: 1. D   2. D   3. (2)   4. C   5. B   6. A   7. C   8. B

18. White Island Visit: 1. C   2. D   3. A   4. C (2, 3, 4, 1)   5. D   6. D   7. B   8. A

19. Bugs Bunny Biography: 1. D   2. B   3. C   4. A   5. B   6. C   7. D   8. A

20. The Photograph: 1. B   2. C   3. D   4. C   5. A   6. D   7. B   8. A

Continued on the next page...

21. Beyond the Black Stump: 1. A   2. D   3. B   4. C   5. D   6. A   7. C   8. B

22. Andy's Gone with Cattle: 1. C   2. A   3. B   4. D   5. A   6. C   7. D   8. C

23. What are Electric Ants? 1. C   2. C   3. B   4. D   5. B   6. A   7. D   8. A

24. The Reconnoitre: 1. A   2. C   3. D   4. A   5. B   6. C   7. D   8. shuffled

25. Ho Chi Minh Mausoleum: 1. B   2. D   3. C   4. B   5. A   6. C   7. B   8. D

26. Bring Back the Rubbish: 1. D   2. helicopter   3. C   4. A   5. D   6. B   7. A   8. B

27. Idioms: 1. D   2. C   3. A   4. B   5. worked   6. C   7. A   8. B

28. How to Write Descriptive Passages: 1. smell   2. D   3. C   4. B   5. D   6. A   7. B   8. C

29. Night Mystery: 1. C   2. A   3. B   4. D   5. B   6. D   7. A   8. C

30. Angkor Wat: 1. C   2. D   3. A   4. B   5. B   6. C   7. A   8. D

31. Book Covers: 1. C   2. B   3. D   4. C   5. A   6. D   7. A   8. C

32. Historic Houses: 1. A   2. False   3. B   4. (2, 4, 1, 3)   5. A   6. D   7. C   8. C

33. Make a Seismometer: 1. B   2. D   3. A   4. C   5. A   6. B   7. C   8. (4, 1, 3, 2)

34. How a Canyon is Formed: 1. D   2. A   3. A   4. D   5. B   6. C   7. B   8. D

35. Segways: 1. A   2. B   3. C   4. D   5. left   6. D   7. B   8. A

36. Understanding Clouds: 1. D   2. B   3. C   4. A   5. C   6. B   7. D   8. B

37. Clichés: 1. C   2. A   3. D   4. B   5. C   6. D   7. D   8. A

38. The Gymnast: 1. B   2. course, route, direction, path   3. C   4. A   5. D   6. D   7. C   8. B

39. Southern Oscillation Index: 1. A   2. D   3. B   4. (2, 1, 4, 3)   5. C   6. farmers   7. A   8. D

40. After the Chase: 1. A   2. B   3. C   4. D   5. C   6. D   7. B   8. A

Understanding Year 7 Comprehension
A. Horsfield © Five Senses Education © W. Marlin

Year 7 Answers

Lit Tips Exercises

No. Text title	Topic	Answers
1. Deep Beyond the Reef	*than* or *then*	1. then (adverb) 2. than (preposition)
2. Green Ants of North Queensland	Irregular plurals	lives, oxen, people; pence, data, sheep, lice; mothers-in-law, bases, deer; child, crisis, fungus
3. Bosley	idiom	got it right, go to bed, crazy
4. The Earthquake	The royal *we*	important (or grand or serious)
5. Canning Stock Route	Shades of meaning	Examples: sobbed, bawled
6. Gumleaf Playing	Euphemisms	1. bald 2. died 3. a quack (suggestion)
7. Terms for Dying	Rhetorical questions	It will never happen!
8. Great Fire of London	Tone in text	foreboding
9. Elimination Tournaments	Suffix *ee*	escapee, divorcee, deportee, employee, addressee, invitee
10. Pigeon Houses	Dashes	No response required.
11. Tidy Towns Scheme	Portmanteau words	smoke/fog, gigantic/enormous, lion/tiger, electronic/mail, sky/peer, chuckle/snort
12. Book Review *Kangaroo*	Short words	refrigerator, zoological garden, taxicab, omnibus, application, caravan
13. Meanings Change	Singular verbs	1. chases 2. grazes 3. fires 4. sees
14. The Brook	Assonance	For men may come and men may go
15. Playing Dominoes	Regular/irregular verbs	ride, write, say, send sold, threw, won, brought, left
16. Pulp Fiction	inverted commas	1. 'friend' 2. 'assistance'
17. Lake Taupo	Irony	No response required.
18. White Island Visit	Brackets	(SCC)
19. Bugs Bunny Bio'	The suffix *ism*	Buddhism, truism, favouritism
20. The Photograph	Mood (atmosphere)	threatening

Continued on the next page...

No.	Text title	Topic	Answers
21.	Beyond the Black Stump	The @ symbol	Responses will vary.
22.	Andy's Gone with Cattle	Genre types	Responses will vary.
23.	Electric Ants	Shades of meaning	Suggestions: serene, calm
24.	The Reconnoitre	Italics	1. *gato* 2. *Star Wars*
25.	Ho Chi Minh Mausoleum	Improving narratives 1	feel/touch, smell, taste, hear touch
26.	Bring Back the Rubbish	Improving narratives 2	hearing (sound)
27.	Idiom	The ellipsis	Habib thought and thought . . .and then thought some more.
28.	How to Write Descriptive Passages	Metonyms	1. ears 2. crown
29.	Night Mystery	Word connotations	acting foolishly, rainbow from moonlight
30.	Angkor Wat	Noun-verb agreement	is, was, remain, seem, has
31.	Book Covers	Know the difference	Responses will vary. B
32.	Historic Houses	Adjective types	third, junior, African, their, dirty, bare
33.	Make a Seismometer	Colons	Jill: To get some water.
34.	How a Canyon is Formed	Adjectives for comparison	worst, least, more, farthest
35.	Segways	Apostrophes	Hey! How is Harry going to get to here if it is raining?
36.	Cloud Symbols	Noun-verb agreement	1. is 2. requires 3. causes 4. helps
37.	Clichés	Clichés	1D, 2C, 3A, 4B, very quickly
38.	The Gymnast	Improving narratives 3	taste
39.	South Oscill. Index	Know the differences (names)	nickname, pen name (or pseudonym or nom de plume)
40.	After the Chase	The prefix *be*	1. behead, beloved, belated 2. begone

Understanding Year 7 Comprehension
A. Horsfield © Five Senses Education © W. Marlin

Notes